DANCING PAST THE DARKNESS

DANCING PAST THE DARKNESS

THE GLORY MINDSET

FELIX HALPERN

DESTINY IMAGE® PUBLISHERS, INC.

P.O. Box 310, Shippensburg, PA 17257-0310

"Promoting Inspired Lives."

This book and all other Destiny Image and Destiny Image Fiction books are available at Christian bookstores and distributors worldwide.

For more information on foreign distributors, call 717-532-3040.

Reach us on the Internet: www.destinyimage.com.

ISBN 13 TP: : 978-0-7684-7423-7
ISBN 13 eBook: 978-0-7684-7424-4

For Worldwide Distribution, Printed in Colombia.

1 2 3 4 5 6 7 8 / 27 26 25 24 23

ACKNOWLEDGMENTS

I want to recognize God's faithfulness and steady hand guiding me into unchartered waters following my crossing over in September 2019. The privilege of returning from death, only to be before the Throne, has carried with me to this day. Carrying the glory and message of Heaven is a blazing torch until the end of my days.

The faithfulness of my wife, Bonnie, who experienced the transformations when a spouse died and returned, is incomprehensible. She, along with my family, are swept down a stream never navigated before. They found strength in Him, sustenance in the daily work of the Spirit.

Not the least, it was a joy working with the teams at Destiny Image and Sid Roth. There is an atmosphere of end-time kingdom purposes. All are deeply impassioned for the glory and the kingdom. I so appreciate the cooperation of Warren Marcus, whose advice helped me bring this work to a fitting close; Shaun Tabatt, for his dedication, encouragement, and heart of servanthood.

Lord, thank you for all the voices and advice that solidified this writing assignment for Your glory.

CONTENTS

FOREWORD

SHE STAYED UP WELL PAST MIDNIGHT, CONVERSING WITH God, petitioning Him. Not a single day passes when she doesn't stand on the side of truth and righteousness. This new end-time soldier bride has found the glory. As her feet have now been shod with the gospel of peace, forged in iron, and stature of maturity, she stands as a well-trained soldier.

This soldier bride is a new harvest of believers with a determination to exercise ancient faith in the ancient one, and to believe again in the possible. It's the end-time Kingdom Normalcy coming out of a long hibernation, and she is going long for the Glory in the end-time harvest of souls. A bride is rising out of the sea with a sword in her hand, and a scroll in the other. Yet her authority will be seen through her humility and servanthood.

Learn how to adjoin yourself to the rising Kingdom and Glory, against the coming storms, and live the life that the bride of Messiah was intended to live!

PREFACE

My name is Rabbi Felix Halpern, and I want to introduce you to a more excellent glory presence life, that grew out of my death and miracle return from the third heaven. But also, I must introduce you to the glory authority that you have over the devil when you discover the glory mindset as your default.

September of 2019 started it all. The brakes were slammed on my life and everything came to a screeching halt. I passed through a heart attack by a doctor's error, died and passed through the spiritual realms, only to find myself in the third heaven face-to-face with the throne. But once your life ends, and your spirit crosses over the great divide, the earth is made naught but for a heavenly residue that sticks to you. Yes, a glorious sticky residue. I can't say it in any other way.

I have always wanted to share my journey in real-time as it unfolds. So, this second work, and the devotional accompanying it, takes you on the second leg of the journey of how the Glory is directing one's daily life. This work proclaims from the mountain tops a crucial message for our times; learn to live life as a Dance, footing past the growing darkness and the stormy atmosphere of our times.

Spending over two decades in the diamond and gold business, some of the most valuable gems have passed through my fingers, even ones uncut rough-looking with no apparent beauty. But one diamond can be worth more than an entire stone quarry, as one loadstone has more virtue than mountains of earth. Our journey together is a little like finding that diamond in the rough. *Dancing Past the Darkness* shares straightforward steps toward that end, and what dropped out of Heaven followed by two life-changing years.

Friend, living life is one thing, but dancing through life is entirely different, particularly when one has the Glory authority. As many experiences can incite change in life, I hope this book prompts a seismic shift in you—something that leaves more room for Him. So, walk slowly here.

There are two kinds of walks we can take here: A lovely walk along a sandy beach, and as the sun rises, take in the sights and sounds of the waves crashing on the shoreline, or something more intentional. Perhaps a kind of walk with a metal detector in our hands.

Although it's a narrower path, and you will navigate between old fallen branches of thought and stones that may obstruct your way, eventually you'll find that diamond in the rough. In other words, don't just read this book. Make it a journey and an adventure.

INTRODUCTION

ANYONE STRUGGLING FOR SPIRITUAL POWER IN A WORLD that is taxed with heaviness and instability, *Dancing Past the Darkness* is for you. Never in 45 years of faith do I remember seeing so much hopelessness in people. From the church's decline in power, she can no longer be the mediating institution and the mitigator that she once was. Without signs and wonders, a lack of discipleship, and the sheer absence of the presence, only exacerbates the problems for God's people.

Now, with a call to action and change, you'll discover again who you are, but also what you are. But the most astounding discovery will be your authority over the devil. In my own journey out of Heaven and the spiritual realms, my former concepts on the actual demise of the devil and his demons changed. I witnessed what it means to have third heaven authority over second heaven principalities. However, I found an unexplained exhilaration as I began to live it, and found life under an open heaven. Each day became a daily adventure.

I know that life is pressure-filled. At times we can be cast as a warrior like David in a dystopian world. Like the Chosen One in a spiritual trope, facing our giants and seasons of trial. In some respects, this writing was my giant and uneasy charge. When I finished my first writings, *A Rabbi's Journey to Heaven* and *Heaven's Soul Cleanse,* there was no way to tie off what had occurred. I was compelled to go further. Seemingly, God stretched His hand toward me with a pen and said, go scribe, tell more of what you have seen and lived through. Now in an expansive view of the glory with the accompanying devotional, a new authority is discovered, as the Glory has been my companion since my return from Heaven.

This second work will not be tentative as was the first. Hopefully, it will cause you to shrug off the cold of the world as you hit the warmth of the glory. Perhaps, think of floating downstream and being lost on the surface of the water, uncaring about where it takes you. I want you to see the purity amid the corruption, the clarity amongst the confusion, and a lost soul standing on the corner, but not for a bus ride to a shopping mall, but for a ticket to Heaven. These of the beautiful takeaways that you can put in your pocket like a coin, and carry with you into your life.

Can you release yourself in that way? If you can, you will learn to live more solidified in His love and glory, and you'll find yourself *Dancing Past the Darkness* of life. The Glory will engulf you, and you will sense a sky overhead, no longer that ceiling feel in your life.

ACQUIRING RIGHT KNOWLEDGE

Many who have read my first writings and continue to do so—*A Rabbi's Journey to Heaven* and *Heaven's Soul Cleanse*—has found it to be head-turning. Personally, my two years of the Soul Cleanse were unrelenting, as I never let myself off for a rest. It hooked me, because I knew I was approaching my soul differently than I was ever taught. If you've read these two works, you'll find a degree of familiarity in this work.

But this new work, *Dancing Past the Darkness,* requires the right knowledge to release its full benefit. For instance, the Glory cannot operate when one believes that miracles ended with the apostles or sickness is God's will. Or God doesn't heal anymore because we are in a different dispensation.

Further, when church leaders openly attribute many of their problems to the devil, it's like a stream of dark informants stealing away the authority from God's people. These are Glory robbers. I see the enemy constantly raising its flag in the House of God, and the devil is mounting gun ports in the House of God, shooting the people of God in their own house. This feverish hammering is impertinent as leaders.

Many do not believe in the Baptism of the Holy Ghost, signs and wonders, and gifts of *dunamis* power. Many believe that born-again believers can be demon possessed—and Satan and his demons can oppress them and be the cause and effect of every problem. This is a gross annihilation of power and Biblically incorrect. The early apostles and the church, never believed these things. Friend, right knowledge is the vessel that allows the Glory to flow, and the Glory is part of our inheritance on earth. We will discuss this at length later in the book. But get ready to open a window. You're about to go down Alice's rabbit hole.

WALKING IN MESSIAH'S FOOTSTEPS

For several months I studied Messiah's footsteps. It felt genuine and real, almost as if I was walking behind Him and following every step He took. As He walked with His early disciples, they walked in the spirit as an end-time warrior bride. They operated in and through the Glory, much like we are supposed to. Yet, they contended with evil, demons and those oppressed too. They knew their authority, and the demons knew them.

When Yeshua fought the devil, the Glory surrounded Him. When He taught the Pharisees in Matthew 12 about demons, the Glory surrounded Him. He gave specific instructions to His disciples about casting out the strong man. He empowered 75 hand-chosen individuals to go and exercise their new authority over demons. They returned excited that the name of Yeshua has all authority over every demonic principality. For this reason, I have included crucial chapters devoted to this Glory Authority.

You see, like the early disciples, we too, are pressing and contending for glory in a world ruled by the prince and the power of the air. These two are inseparable. Kingdom power is an amalgam of glory and authority. Without knowledge, authority is elusive. Even demons have knowledge that Christians lack today. *"And the evil spirit answered and said unto them, Jesus I know, and Paul I know; but who are ye?"* (Acts 19:15 KJV). Therefore, we must learn again what the devil can do and what he cannot do. This was something that the disciples knew well.

After you read this book, there will be no more fever-ish hammering from the devil or his demons. No conflict from Satan's harbor, or feeling as a prisoner trying to escape. You will never let your guard down again to the multitude of Glory robbers. If the Glory is to operate and remain, we must marry knowledge with power, knowledge with Glory. Yeshua was the consummate Glory God-man and teacher. This mighty compact of Glory with knowledge is invincible.

Accompanying this work is a 30-day devotional and journal to help deepen your adventure in *Dancing Past the Darkness*. Practical Kingdom-centered activities are offered to align your life with Kingdom Normalcy, and find daily practices to bring freedom from earthly pressures. One will mimic life in revival. Your soul will be free from the weight of earthly things, no longer just looking at the crashing waves upon the shore, but observing an ageless dance throughout your day.

1

MEET YOUR DANCE PARTNER

IT WOULD SEEM IN ORDER BEFORE LEARNING THE LIFE OF Dancing Past the Darkness to meet your dance partner. If one has no flame of love, it's like hobbling to the dance floor, leaving with disappointment. You keep expecting to see change and feel something new, but you'll be limping away.

When a man and a woman dance, they are positioned physically close. They see each other eye to eye, obtaining affection from one another. When I met my wife over forty-five years ago, I remember the beat of my heart every day that I was going to be with her. Dating was an exciting time. It became more exciting and lovely when we decided to spend our lives together. Something ignites inside of you called First Love.

Later, when my daughter was getting married, I took dance lessons to perform the father-of-the-bride dance with utmost efficiency. When Bonnie and I stepped into the dance studio for our classes, we were removed from all thoughts of the world. It was magical. Both of us felt captivated while listening to the instructor. I want you to see your Lord similarly. Let's get closer, eyeball to eyeball with Yeshua, and be captivated again by the Bridegroom.

THE BRIDEGROOM

God is more than that big church with a white dome and beautiful windows. You know that, right? Sabbath is more than a day off and a religious gathering. Sabbath is an appointment to meet with God. One also does not need to try hard to save one's soul; it comes with a simple step of faith by asking the Lord to come into your life. And if the candle of the Lord can stay alight in you, you won't be joining in the noisy throng of this world ever again.

Dancing Past the Darkness is also easy, if your heart is willing. Salvation. Suppose you need it. Take that step of faith to ask the Lord to come into your life. "Lord, I ask that You come into my life, that Jesus, Yeshua, the Jewish Messiah, become my King and Lord and forgive me of my sins." Once that step of faith is done, a spiritual marriage occurs.

ARISE! IT'S MORNING

When I think of His love, Romans 8:38-39 (NKJV) rises in me:

> *I am persuaded that neither death nor life, nor angels nor principalities nor powers, nor things present nor things to come, nor height nor depth, nor any other created thing, shall be able to separate us from the love of God which is in Christ Jesus our Lord.*

His mercy falls every morning, softening the hardened places of my heart, and the edges of a harsh world seem to disappear. His steadfast love is the parent of faithfulness, and they preserve us. "HE" is dependable, loyal, all-loving, never selfish, and always giving of Himself—He is everything a bride wants from her Groom. He never trips us up; He is always nimble, moving and guiding us, knowing every emotion every second. Nothing can separate us from the Love of God. Many of us can identify with this picture of Him.

Song of Solomon is a gold mine of mediation too. I find two betrothed individuals. In Song of Solomon 3:4 (KJV), which says, *"It was but a little that I passed from them, but I found him whom my soul loveth: I held him, and would not let him go, until I had brought him into my mother's house, and into the chamber of her that conceived me."* Fathom the deep connection here: Marriage, union, oneness, intimacy. It beckons us to come closer.

Dancing Past the Darkness may start this way. When that morning dawns, and you are about to start another day, the previous day's storms have hopefully abated. Start your day a little earlier to begin more peacefully. Take time to wait for Him and incline your ear to His words, so that you enter the day with a glory mindset. But when every morning begins: He says, blessed is the man or woman who makes Him his trust; the one who does not go the way of the proud or chases after a lie. I often see the Lord high and lifted. Only to remind me that He has given us an open ear, constantly extending a solid willing hand. God says, "I delight in those who want to draw close to Me, so walk with Me and dance." He says, "I look to and fro for those who take pleasure in ME."

Where are they?

You, my beloved, are my delight. And if I haven't mentioned it, put a notebook down on that tiny table where you usually put your coffee and Bible. Journal your time when you're *Dancing Past the Darkness.* Your memories will remain untouched by time, and you'll return to them.

THE GREATEST LOVE STORY

Let's rehearse our story.

Now that we're married to our Bridegroom and waiting for the marriage supper of the Lamb, it's still the most incredible love story ever told, sung and lived. Our Father sent His only Son to capture our not Love because He wanted a relationship with us. "Take me away with you—let us hurry! Let the king bring me into his chambers." Friends, we rejoice and delight in Him, and we will praise Him whose love is sweeter than wine.

How right we are to adore Him! (Song of Solomon 1:4)

Why is it that such words come when we think of our Groom?

Why is it that such thoughts flood our souls? Because our soul is captivated. God has ambushed us. Remember?

Two thousand years ago, Yeshua came to earth to stand by our side out of love. It was the first kind of love rooted in self-sacrifice, freely offered, and desiring nothing in return. As a Jew, I came to the knowledge of my Messiah, as historically, we as a people have longed for a descendant of David. One who would be a prophet like David in which God would speak to Israel again as in the days of old. This longing was projected into a time called the latter days, and fulfilled two thousand years ago through our Jewish Messiah, Yeshua, Jesus.

We also have ingrained in us a godlike hero or leader who personifies the ideals and values we all cherish. For this, the Son of God came to earth willingly and not sparingly, leaving behind Heaven's glories to be born into an ordinary family with no material means.

He was born of the line of David through royal descent; He was the actual prophesied Jewish Messiah. He lived a simple life that knew the sweat of the brow. He made the helpless and hopeless His friends. He had compassion for those abandoned by society, scarred by disease and rejection. When Yeshua came, it was a promise fulfilled by His Father:

> *"Do not fear; your God will come...he will come to save you." Then will the eyes of the blind be opened and the ears of the deaf unstopped. Then will the lame leap like a deer, and the mute tongue shout for joy* (Isaiah 35:3-6).

In the Talmud, written 500 years before the birth of Yeshua, they said, *"When the Messiah comes, He will sit among the poor and the suffering sick. He will be wounded healer—One who will first carry our sickness to bring us healing"* (Sanhedrin 98a). Once again, from the words of Isaiah in chapter 53:4-5 (ESV):

Surely he has borne our griefs and carried our sorrows...He was pierced for transgressions [sins] and crushed for iniquities; upon him was the chastisement [punishment] that brought us peace, and with his wounds we are healed.

He showed us that God had not forgotten or abandoned us to our miseries. He revealed the depth of God's favor on us despite our failures. He was teaching us to believe that the God of the universe hears every word from our hearts. He promised us peace of mind, and planted in our inmost being the seeds of hope—that someday we would be liberated from this body of sin, and taken home to be with Him forever. Also, to have a blessed life of joy here too. Finally, He revealed to us the depth and the width of God's immeasurable love when Yeshua was crucified on our behalf by taking our place. But the story did not end there.

When people hear this love story two thousand years later, they cry, confess their sins, ask for forgiveness, and they are filled with joy and assurance. When one meets Yeshua for the first time, they can swallow down the hurt within them; the wash of painful memories is swept away. So yes, it's about relationship, love, and fire.

Do you have it, or have you lost it?

LOSS OF FIRST LOVE

Given our discussion, what happens when one loses First Love? First, you know you have stepped away from your Dance Partner. The result is painful. You're vanquished of the heavenly emotion that once filled you. "His" presence is now a distant memory as you go through the outward motions, but a cold feeling has taken hold of your soul. Every day is lived in the shadow of what was. And even though "His" steady gaze remains because HE is faithful, HE is waiting to reach out with His love, still, you are cold and indifferent.

As time goes on, you look in the mirror and you notice the sparkle in your eye is gone. It's been replaced with a sparkle for the world again.

Have you noticed the spiritual disease of amnesia that has taken hold, where you forgot everything excellent and lovely? Little by little, your soul offloads the beautiful experiences that came to define your life. This is a deep misfortune, because where love and fire are the foundation for passion, passion becomes our purpose when we use it in God's Kingdom.

For this reason, losing First Love is so grievous to God.

Many leaders have lost their First Love too. Perhaps you're one. You are caught in a sudden flash of a moment. Silence. You are standing still, slowly and carefully, running through your mind how you got here. It is easy to become a spiritual professional, executive—CFO, COF, CEO—in our organized corporate ministry world today. It's easy to join the ranks of spiritual bureaucrats and spiritual corporate titans, where professionality trumps Glory. Church growth models trump presence-driven initiatives, and motivational speakers rally the sheep. Today, a church or congregation can operate like any finely tuned business enterprise, but for all practical purposes, the fire is gone.

Have you grown weary?

Is the excitement of winning a lost soul a vague memory?

Pause! Pray! Repent! Ask the Lord to restore the fire you once had because it's hard to serve God with your total energy and commitment when First Love is gone.

I cannot help but repeatedly think of the Ephesian Church:

> *Yet I hold this against you: You have forsaken the love you had at first. Consider how far you have fallen! Repent and do the things you did at first. If you do not repent, I will come to you and remove your lampstand from its place* (Revelation 2:4-5).

REMEMBER WHEN?

The apostle Paul demonstrates that everything came from the ethos (character, attitude, spirit) he experienced on the Damascus Road. It was so powerful and life-changing that it defined him as a trustworthy servant, solidly rooted in his convictions.

In other words, how has your life changed through the character of Yeshua, and His principles of the Kingdom? What is the strength of your convictions that determines the veracity of your authority? Can you take a moment and recall the day?

For most, our *ethos* was formed from the intensity of our first encounter with faith. We might call it the "fire regulator." I was brought back to my first encounter when I saw

Paul's, and I wanted more! This is what Paul does for us. We want more and desire to reignite a fire in us.

> Paul states it flawlessly, "I press toward the mark." Paul is dancing like you and I daily, struggling to get someplace new with God as we are doing together here.

Pressing in comes with intentionality. Yet, many relinquish this holy duty of pressing in. Often one's pressing is no more than the ebb and flow of the current swaying against coral on a coral reef. That is not pressing in. That's just existing! Paul's pressing in is motivated by intention because of hope for more.

I mentioned early in the book that as tradition can suck the oxygen out of interest, institutional religion and denominationalism leave little room to question and search too. You sit back and rest, but do not ponder your next Abrahamic step. Instead, you languish in what you know and have been given.

The soul is thirsty. It needs to drink constantly. It's part of our unique "life force," because it's how we were created. We want to get to that place where we are waiting for Him again as one in the lobby of a hotel in the morning. Standing away from the door with our backs turned to anyone coming who might block our view.

Oh yes, friend! He is real. I can only picture us flying up to the clouds with Him , and flying away far off over the ocean and flying away, far off over the ocean—which is my dream for you. Beyond the sea begins the land of our Creator, of everything good, right and lovely. And it is here, beloved, that we gather at the jump-off point. Climb out of the confines of the room, go to the window, and jump through, journey down into Alice's rabbit hole, for His Love is worth it.

2

DANCING PAST THE DARKNESS

And hath raised us together and made us
sit together in heavenly places in Yeshua
(Ephesians 2:6 KJV).

WHAT IS IT?

You're about to jump into the day. But in contrast to Dancing Past the Darkness, it's impossible to envision how the day will go or end. None of us can. It may not be that charming mixture that you wanted, because the world is an expansive display of cold and harsh realities.

Still, joy can strike your cheeks knowing that every morning is a day filled with good and pleasant surprises. The key is knowing scales of importance, which we speak at length about later, because it deserves greater attention. Learn to let go of unimportant things so as not to hemorrhage spiritual and emotional power and strength. Learn to detach from these robbers of time and peace that are around every corner. Change the subject of your focus and thoughts.

I realize in this book with the devotional that follows, how much I need to talk about the stewarding of the soul. If for no other reason than to provide a release valve for the pressure that's building inside so many.

Dancing Past the Darkness is one way to release the pressure as it came directly out of the glory side, Heaven. Those revelations from the third heaven, and where daily struggles were eased upon my return. Now that I am grounded in a greater sense of eternalness, I notice God's handprint throughout the day. I see how trees cling to the darkness, almost holding on to the night a bit longer. I see these slight nuances in life because I admire His creation's glory. It is a product of our Creator and the life of *Dancing Past the Darkness.*

Like so many, I raced past things like everyone else before the Glory side. Now it only takes seconds to spot something to marvel at. In the hot stream of people and things to do, God puts His hand on my shoulder, and I feel Heaven saying, "It's okay! Dance more, you are not of this world. Look and see what I want to do with you today." I want this for you, and it is the purpose of this writing.

Of course, there is no quick magic formula for this. Patterns of thinking and habits don't die quickly, do they? But with straightforward steps to guide us, seasoned with a bit of desperation and the power of the Holy Spirit, a profound revival is possible in one's life.

The first step is to see differently, perhaps like a jeweler's trained eye with a jeweler's glass in hand. Let's learn to admire more of our Creator's work. That doesn't seem too tricky, right? Psalm 8:4 (ESV) states, *"What is man that you are mindful of him...?"* From this passage, we think of our smallness in the shadow of God's greatness.

> God tells us plainly what we are. The tiniest grain of sand is not so small to the whole Earth as man is to Heaven. Yet, man in his pride sees no such greatness other than in himself.

WHAT IS MAN?

The Hebrew word for man here is enosh. It is an expression not of power or strength but frailty and fragility. That poses a choice. One can live in the shadow of one's abilities, intellect, and successes, or God's greatness, holiness and presence.

Man is acutely dwarfed in the light of His Glory and power. Yet, he always sees himself as more vital than he is. Quickly to flatter himself, one man to flatter another, he espouses words of wisdom, yet he knows not which way the wind will blow from one moment to another. Some dreams are fulfilled, and some are not. Bad and good years come; hardship and plenty, celebration and sadness. But we learn how limited our life is to the rapidity of time. Twisting, and turning, the span of years stretches out only to realize what eludes us in our youth—our fragility.

So, what is a man then, O Lord?

A vapor, gone in the morning?

When his time is up, he is gone?

Nothing more and nothing less, it seems.

But a conundrum is found here that can only be answered by God Himself. The Lord says that man is My creation. Out of nothingness and from mere dust, I formed him. I gave him My spirit and stored it in a soul and a biological body that I knit together. I created him in My image that my thoughts miraculously become his thoughts. That man's ways become My ways. Indeed, man is the most privileged of God's creation. Eternity is reserved for us alone, a promise of living in this spiritual wonder, where everything is timeless and joy is overflowing. Majesty beyond comprehension! A life saturated in the abundance of My glorious rain.

What is a man, then? A token of My love, says God.

A channel of My presence. Something wonderfully made and miraculously born of nothing. Yes, we are miracles, divinely set in life on paths determined by our Creator. Waiting to be clothed in an eternal garment that shall never fade—held each day in His hand. We look to the heavens to thank Him for the breath that gave us life. We are incomprehensible!

SENSING GOD'S HANDIWORK

Now that we tasted merely one thumbprint-sized piece of marvelousness, pause to consider the colossal-sized environment of Heaven in all its glory. Imagine. Heaven can comfortably hold all the redeemed, past, present, and future. Wrap your mind around that alone?

I saw in Heaven an endless stream of light from His presence emanating from the throne. Of course, every power has its source, and in Heaven, all luminance comes from our Creator. We have these words in Isaiah 60:19, *"The sun will no more be your light by day, nor will the moon's brightness shine on you, for the LORD will be your everlasting light, and your God will be your glory."* Also, from Revelation 22:5: *"There will be no more night. They will not need the light of a lamp or the sun's light, for the Lord God will give them light. And they will reign forever and ever."*

Steady light streams sparkled from the waters by the river's surface. I stood by this timeless envelope, with a golden hue above this glorious habitation cast over the vast firmament above. And if it were not for me inured through the sacrifice of His Son, I couldn't have crossed over from the mortal realm.

In Heaven, time doesn't exist as days and years as on earth. You are in a conscious state of eternal bliss nested in an unending time window. When your final *stop* occurs, you pace quickly through the golden streets marveling at this majestic life. I saw the redeemed making their way according to their pleasure dictates. They enjoy one another with joy and worry-free living.

The light surrounding me was brighter than anything I remember in the mortal realm. The colors were vibrant with a perceivable depth. The water of the river that I stood by was effervescent. My hearing was acutely sensitive as I could hear different spectrums of sound simultaneously.

Still, it was not befuddling as standing in the middle of 5th Avenue at noon, or in the Bronx in a swarm of people, cars, and elevated trains racing by. My sense of smell experienced a pure freshness of the creation within Heaven. One's senses are *fully* alive. I never experienced that in the mortal realm. And make no mistake, your feelings play an integral part in seeing the glory of God here.

That's what it's all about in our study—getting our eyes drawn to God's majesty the same way David looks to the heavens, the sun, the moon, and the stars. He said, "consider the heavens, sky, and its beauty; a starry night as the evening is a glow under the light of a full moon." He breaks into this sense of humble admiration for God and marvels at his world. The grandeur against the littleness; the excellence against the corruption; the majesty against man's meanness. We're getting our senses queued for the Glory.

Do you sense it?

It's about finding more pleasure in a day, enjoying God, and maintaining permanence and transformation. Like walking on a road with no end, only for your foot to come down on something that catches your eye, and there it is. His handprint.

If you travel above the earth to the highest star where new planets and systems are spotted, He is there. Never will one exhaust the limits of His dominion. In John 1:3 (NKJV), *"All things were made through him, and without him was nothing made...."* And Psalm 115:16 (ESV), *"The heavens are the LORD's heavens, but the earth he has given to the children of man."* Trek into the deepest forest, never walked by a man before. You will see Him. Look up to the heavens and marvel at the natural order of life, which goes unnoticed daily. The well-known saying that "Beauty lies in the eyes of the beholder" is true. It depends on your heart and mind. I say it depends upon Glory eyes.

> **Everything has beauty in our Father's world, but not everyone sees it. The unbeliever sees God in nothing, and the child of God sees God in everything.**

As David meditates on the heavens, sky, and its beauty (Psalm 19:1-6), it is believed that he wrote Psalm 19:1-6 while envisioning them in his morning prayer. He saw a double kind of knowledge, another book of all that the Creator gave to us. "The heavens declare," to make men declare the Glory of God, by their admiration and marvel.

To God's people, nature is a natural preaching in every language.

> *For since the creation of the world God's invisible qualities—his eternal power and divine nature— have been clearly seen, being understood from what has been made, so that people are without excuse* (Romans 1:20).

It is in this context that I want you to enjoy the sky above you again, and then you will see the ground different from before.

3

VERTICAL/ HORIZONTAL LIVING

ALTHOUGH TIME IS ORIENTED HORIZONTALLY OR LIN-early, our relationship with God is vertical. Horizontal living is flat, driven by tradition and the convention of natural life. It is non-relational. It is like a train moving across the ground on its track; people get on and off but rarely does anyone take the time to know someone. People walk by each other without taking notice of the slightest nuance of each other. Although this flat existence shares common space with others, as on a bus, a train, a church, a restaurant, or an event, people never slow down long enough to look up (get vertical) and see what's around and above them. This is flat living.

For 25 years, I commuted on a bus to New York City. Men had identical tan-style raincoats carrying Samsonite brief-cases. I always had an aversion to that. In some cases, it's the way it was from one generation to the next. Sons followed their fathers, and rarely was time taken to question and consider something different.

In this flat orientation, everything is streaming across the flat course of life, denying adventure and surprise by being tone-deaf and unsighted to the sounds and sights beyond the apparent daily routine. Horizontal/flat living is driven by our carnal and soulish desires, shaped by how we think our life should be.

Vertical living is plumb with Heaven, and is an axiom of spiritual living that Jesus calls us to by letting Him shape, and define our lives. Kingdom, or vertical living is reaching up into the glory, or in Hebrew, *shamayim,* the heavens. It's dimensional. Because the Divine is more involved daily, we're more conscious of His involvement in our daily life.

> You see, it is not only how much God wants to activate in you; it's how much you want God to activate in you.

As this vertical living takes hold, we start to savor moments, places, and people. Spiritual and Glory inferences are newly exposed. Life becomes more dimensionally oriented and enjoyable. It seems boring now to only observe the outward nature of things, never pausing to peer out beyond the obvious.

Instead of merely appreciating the beauty of that flower, why not stop to examine the inside? It is having conversations with people and listening instead of words going in one ear and out the other: listening, learning, receiving, and making eye contact. SLOW down, *stop,* and let your God-given senses reward you with more pleasure.

YOU HAVE THE EYES TO SEE IT

My senses operated optimally in Heaven, so I returned with them supercharged. As Heaven surrounded me, I marveled at a carousel of glorious pleasures. These pleasures and desires have not left me, as vertical living has taken hold. I am convinced that NDE (Near-Death Encounter) or ALS (After-Life Survivors) return to enjoy a greater range of their senses. A lingering gift for the suffering before I died. We stop to admire objects around us that would have previously eluded us. We want to help others learn, slow down, and enjoy what God has given us. I want to help you find the surprises in front of you, as well as above and around you. Get into the habit of turning your head to the side and up. Go beyond the common usage of sight, smell, taste, touch, and hearing. See how many new discoveries you can find.

Get dimensional!

THE MIRACLE OF SIGHT

Consider the following: People with normal vision can see a grapefruit 1,250 feet away, a small print within inches of their nose. A hawk's distance vision is better than ours in daylight, but his eyes don't have the range ours do after the sun goes down. A honeybee can see more than we can up close, but his distance seeing is terrible compared with a human's. We can perceive distant objects 100 times smaller than those a honeybee can.

Our ability to perceive color is among the best in the animal kingdom. Ostriches can discriminate among colors, and even fish can tell all the rainbow colors. But the human eye could distinguish hundreds of thousands of variations in shades of color, far too many to have individual names. Some living creatures hunt by day, but are blind at night. Another group can't see well by day—these hunt at night. The human eye is very adaptable, it can get see by day and reasonably well by night. Our eyes have a visual intensity range of one billion to one; we can see by the glaring light of a tropical sun or the dimmest starlight, at least to some extent.[1]

So, why don't we discover and enjoy more?

Flat living. Busyness. Distraction. Wrong orientation.

We are living in the wrong universe.

HOUSTON, WE HAVE A PROBLEM

One of my favorite movies is Apollo 13. In its accurate depiction of what happened, Tom Hanks, who plays an astronaut, suddenly sees warning lights going off while on his way to the moon. His famous words: "Houston, we have a problem."

Similarly, "Heaven, we have a problem!"

During the early days of the COVID pandemic, New York City looked like a ghost town. But the air cleared up, and the sky was beautiful again. I remember how white the clouds were, and those beautiful daily sunsets were breathtaking. I can still visualize that time.

Life changed. People were awakened from the flat, horizontal plane overnight. Suddenly, life got dimensional. Neighbors were outside no longer with their cell phones in hand, but with a cup of coffee and their children. Husbands and wives were out together. Neighbors were out and about conversing. People escaped their silos and broke from the flat, robotic life. We don't need to lose this. We can learn from COVID and reclaim a deeper, more enjoyable life built around the simple, cost-free wonders that God gave us.

But many have returned to their silos. The roads are jammed again. The air is dirty. Once again, many have robotically fallen into the world's default mode, which is counterintuitive to a presence-driven life. I remember how I thrived on doing as much, getting as much, and being as much as possible. It's as if a switch has been flipped in me. Now I wonder how I ever wanted any of that life. Now, my dance is too important, my time with my loved ones, nature, lost souls, feeding my "soul" with manna from Heaven.

I don't want to be subtle here. I care too much for you. And even though every part of me is questioning how to fix this mess before it gets completely out of control, desperation is the seed bed to break the cycle for God to release revival rains.

BREAK THE CYCLE

Dancing Past the Darkness can be like dancing on a high-speed moving train, because life is busy and intensely demanding. But my lips actually part with the words *intent* to come out. I sit contemplating this book with at times tears welling up in my eyes knowing the hour that we are in and the need for God's people to be strong.

Dancing Past the Darkness is about intentionally living life in the slow lane. Consider the words from Psalm 131:2: *"But I have calmed and quieted myself; I am like a weaned child with its mother; like a weaned child I am content."* We cannot quiet ourselves if the people of God stay conditioned to thrive and crave busyness just like the world. If there is no adequate time for God, how can we nurture our inner environment of our souls?

For instance, one can't plan the Holy Spirit into their day, yet many try. The busyness of life squeezes out the Holy Spirit, as church services are mostly flat too. Most are programmed—ordered—timed, and neatly fit together like pieces in a jigsaw puzzle. The Holy Spirit hates that. Thousands of churches try to plan in the Holy Spirit, and it fails repeatedly. Well, you can try, but you might be dancing alone. There is a vast difference between the Holy Spirit planning you, and you planning the Holy Spirit. For this reason, we cannot allow ourselves to be driven by the cultural stopwatch, as the Bible places high value on rest and peaceful living.

> Romans 12:2 says, "Do not conform to the pattern of this world, but be transformed by the renewing of your mind. Then you will be able to test and approve what God's will is—his good, pleasing, and perfect will."

FIND REST FOR YOUR SOUL

Yeshua often escaped the busyness of the crowds to renew His strength many times. He also needed rest for His soul. Mark 6:31 says, "Because so many people were coming and going that they did not even have a chance to eat, he said to

[His disciples], 'Come with me by yourselves to a quiet place and get some rest.'"

Luke 10:38-42 says:

> *As Jesus and his disciples were on their way, he came to a village where a woman named Martha opened her home to him. She had a sister called Mary, who sat at the Lord's feet listening to what he said. But Martha was distracted by all the preparations that had to be made. She came to him and asked, "Lord, don't you care that my sister has left me to do the work by myself? Tell her to help me!" "Martha, Martha," the Lord answered, "you are worried and upset about many things, but few things are needed—or indeed only one. Mary has chosen what is better, and it will not be taken away from her."*

ESSENTIAL POINTS TO CONSIDER

1. Your time belongs to God and the Kingdom on earth, your children, grandchildren,, and spouse. All else falls below those.

2. We think that our problems deserve a ten rating, and everything is a 911, please call it urgent. Yet, 95 percent of things will work themselves out without worrying. Identify the critical issues that need attention and let the other minuscule things go.

3. You don't always need to know something immediately. Give time her chance to reveal what only time can give—partner with her and experience self-control. Don't obsess over what you do not know.

4. A harsh word from someone lingers in an experience during the day or the last week. If you've ever experienced losing someone—I know many have during COVID, and as my wife, Bonnie, experienced with my death and life—scales of importance shift dramatically. Learn scales of importance.

5. The Kingdom is living simpler and slower. Simpler is living larger. Smaller living is living bigger with more power. Debt-free living is power when one is no longer a servant to the lender. It is not the amount of money one makes, it's the debt service needed to maintain it.

6. The world calls covetousness, ambition. Hoarding, prudence. Greed, industry. This is pressure on your soul and spirit. Less stress equals more room for God, and more time to share the good news in your day.

NOTE

1. https://www.nytimes.com/1964/03/15/archives/we-have-more-than-five-senses-most-people-take-the-faculties-of.html; accessed October 27, 2022.

4

GETTING READY TO DANCE

WE ARE IN A GLORY-CENTERED TIME IN HISTORY, YET IN the center of the storm. It is the eye of the storm however that I want you to take residence in. Sit down in the eye for a moment and look out at everything swirling around you.

One morning God told me to stay in the light and avoid the shadows. Then I was given an action to take, which you will hear more about in a later chapter. But this one action formed the early steps of *Dancing Past the Darkness.* In time, I've manifested this life, spoken into existence, and walked it into my universe. *Dancing Past the Darkness* is going to set a calming hand on your days. Like me, you will be struck by a deep resident hope to pull down all worries, fears, and anxieties under a water-like surface where they never come up again. I hope this is your experience.

OUR TIMES

I admit that the following comments might seem sudden. Still, hopefully, annoyance will not be flitting across some faces, because I don't want to dismiss the negative environment of our times. Everything is not okay down here! When

I look out upon the horizon of our times, my eyes grow strangely intense because more storm clouds are gathering.

So, before we get ready to dance, let's review some things that only increase the comparative advantage of *Dancing Past the Darkness*.

We live in a time when modern-day prophets are quick to judge the world, yet they don't consider themselves, which is a problem. The Church's unfocused vision of the Spirit and its presence is a problem. People's lack of spiritual authority and an acute recession of spiritual power in the Church are abnormal, given the normalcy of the Kingdom seen in the New Testament. Of course, if one believes that miracles ended with the Apostolic period, where the days of miracles are of the past, then what we have is normal. I wondered about how you see things?

I see so many who have lost excitement for the Kingdom, and are no longer interested in pursuing more than what they have experienced in the past. Unwittingly, many are unaware of the spiritual tug of war raging in them, so they have wearied and thrown up their arms, now left only with dreams of when things will change. I find encouragement if my words cause uneasiness in your heart. It means that you understand the thrust of my words.

We are also in a time when man has brought the Glory down to a casual state. Holy things and Holy moves seem mundane, let alone rare, and too many services begin with man and end with man. Preaching strives to be a lecture or a dissertation of some kind. Ministry work has replaced Glory encounters. Ministry awards have replaced divine visitations.

Form and structure have replaced the free-flowing presence of the Spirit. Is this problem found everywhere? Praise God, no. But conventionalists of course, will take issue with my comments. Instead, one should be troubled by the rationalizing of the deep changes in our modern day.

It's been so long since God's people have seen the Glory, our Father's children forgot what the Glory sounds, looks, and smells like. And yes, the Glory has a sound, a look, and a fragrance. Now they are conditioned to wait only for the big bang from Heaven to awaken them because they cannot hear His voice in the stillness.

To make matters worse, millions are coming out of this modern scorpion-like plague, the COVID, like bewildered sheep coming out of a deep forest. Disillusionment is in their eyes, uncertainty torments their soul, because everything that could be shaken shakes our lives. God's people need to rediscover their identity to ensure sustainability as a general statement for the Church.

> So, we must go back to the beginning! Discover how we started! Discover again the love, power, and glory of God!

I know that I am a voice of one calling forth in a desert of dry bones, prepare ye the way of the Lord. Many are also resounding with the same message. Whether it is being proclaimed openly as here and now, or in your hearts where you hear the reverberations of the Spirit inside of you. While

COVID awakened slumbering spirits, it accelerated things that would have been revealed later. It exposed conditions in the Church. It arrested many so they could *stop, spot* their weaknesses, and *swap* for something better. Often, we are *stopped* to *swap* for something better in our lives.

THREE LAST-MINUTE CONCERNS

First: Have you lost your holy curiosity? There are many reasons for this. Living on past glories, past experiences. The status quo and religion will surely do it. They will suck the oxygen out of curiosity. Also, one's past experiences can falsely make one feel like an expert. When a new fire burns, it looks dull because the old fire blocks your way. Some think the former fire and rain is greater than the latter and the present. So, they're not being soaked today. I surmise what is wrong with some is that they're just too set in their ways, unwilling to be removed from their complacency or familiarity.

Can you imagine having a new experience under an unfamiliar rain and fire? I want that question to roll the stone away from the tomb of your past experiences. Now take one leg and lift yourself out of those confines, then visualize a sustainable, more presence-driven life.

Second: *Dancing Past the Darkness* can be like dancing atop a moving train at high speed. But that's okay! Imagine an oasis on top of that train, a stillness in the middle of the hustle of life, a quietness amidst the thrashing sounds of people, planes, trains, and automobiles. I assure you, you will learn to make some adjustments here, but we will need the anointing of the Spirit.

Third: No Lot's-Wife-People Allowed! No Lot's People allowed, and no Noah people who are more interested in buying, selling, and running to and fro, and no frog-in-boiling-water people who are oblivious to our times and their own spiritual apathy. I'm sorry, it just won't work! But you can change. The Holy Spirit can change you.

To go on this journey, no one can look back. You must start your morning with a fresh start—it's a new day! Say to yourself, "I am fortunate to be alive today, because I realize that I have been given the precious gift of life, and I'm going to make this day count for His glory." Yesterday's events are history. The moments ahead are mere steps in the making, and every moment requires its unique action. Each day you'll begin to see every phone call, text, and social media post, not vital to the universe. Every problem isn't critical as it seems, because you're learning to be the guardian of your soul. Everything that comes your way doesn't need your 911 attention.

In this new life, you learn to let some balls fly by because we all know how quickly small things can become large things. We could chase one wind upon another, only to be stirred by something else that swoops down upon us. These are all what I call joy robbers seeking to draw us into their chaotic world. But these glory robbers are not only in the outside world. Knowing scales of importance is key, so there is a colossal shift in scales of importance.

NOW LET'S GET READY TO DANCE

Every chapter now that follows is like learning a new dance step, a new frame of mind, and a fresh inner disposition of your soul. Imagine us standing together at the starting line. You will not begin to learn the comparative advantage of Dancing Past the Darkness to the work of the spirit that is seen in the institutional and conventional church. We're going back to Kingdom Normalcy.

Are you ready?

We're positioned, leaning over, and ready to accelerate onto a new path. Visualize the starting line framed in a beautiful picture, resting alongside a gentle, running stream. Our Groom sits beside us, watching with interest. Like that coin deep in your pocket you carry with you, you are filled with hope for change. For what other reason have we joined together?

Friend, when I'd first conceived my life this way, through the weeks and months and three years that followed, I was footing through my days light and airy during the dark and stormy events of our times. Wonderfully, I had unwavering objectivity following 45 years of knowing the Lord. Now at 70, it seems that an old dog is being taught many new tricks! Old mindsets broke off as the conventional glass began shattering into a thousand pieces. The Holy Spirit became the perfect director, guiding me gently, skillfully, I might add. Now it's going to be your turn to displace some old mindsets and shatter your conventional glass.

5

HEAVEN ON EARTH

LEARN TO DETACH!

Learning to step outside yourself is to stop and be intentionally unrestricted by your day's schedule and activities. You see, the Glory needs elbow room. Not elbow grease because you already have the oil of the Holy Spirit. The problem is in our soul, which is like a crowded street filled with earthly occupations on every side. God showed me how to stop, and start seeing the world that our Father made for us.

I step out to marvel at the sky overhead in the morning. Sometimes no robin sings because I see barren trees in winter. Yet, the red cardinal is easily seen against the virgin snow. In the absence of the house finch that typically makes their presence known, birds of prey are looking for food. Open your eyes to His Glory. It's the way! You can do it!

> Finding a life of admiration for God's greatness is the beginning of a glory mindset and a life of dancing past the darkness.

The Scripture states, *"It is the glory of God to conceal a matter, but the glory of kings is to search out a matter"* (Proverbs 25:2 NKJV). Go out today like those ancient explorers arriving on the shores of an unexplored land.

TIME IS NON-EXISTENT

When I was in Heaven, there were no days, weeks, months, seconds, or minutes. Since my crossing over, I have not worn a watch. To be perfectly honest, I am untethered to time. I get to my appointments promptly. I eat when I am hungry, sleep when I am tired, and wake up when it's time; usually around 3 a.m. I have replaced my watch with a compass to remind me that position is more important than time. Consequently, I have learned to tell time by the position of the sun, and I follow the rhythms of the day and season. Truly, I have become untethered to the mortal realm living the words of Yeshua's, that I am in this world, but not of it.

I encourage you to try it out to experience its freedom. This principle is foreseen in many places in Scripture (see Philippians 3:20; Romans 12:1-2; 1 John 2:15-17; 1 Peter 2:11-12). C.S. Lewis said: "Aim at heaven, and you will get earth thrown in. Aim at earth and you get neither." What I want to introduce you to is the principle of being *detached*. Detachment can also be seen as something negative. The Oxford dictionary defines detachment as a "state of being objective or aloof." But being aloof serves no use. Being objective is acutely beneficial. This is where the discipline of detachment becomes an incredible skill worth learning. It's constantly pushing impermanent areas of life away.

Detachment focuses on those things you have control over, and not what others do or what others say. You focus on how you treat others, your actions and words, the effort you put into something, and how you steward your soul. Yeshua taught on detachment. We are in the world but not of it (John 17:16); that we do not store up treasures where rust and moth destroy (Matthew 6:19); that we do not worry for tomorrow (Matthew 6:34); even HE, our Lord, says to look how He takes care of the lilies of the field (Matthew 6:28).

DETACH FROM THE SHADOWS

I mentioned in the book that God told me to stay in the light and away from the shadows. I have always felt I have done that. I lived for the Lord according to His word. I refused offers when presented with business partnerships, because I could not be unequally yoked. I honored my Sabbaths, gave as I should, lived my life for the Lord, and raised my children for Him.

When it was time to leave my secular work as vice president of a multimillion-dollar company in my mid-forties, the Lord told me to give away my retirement and savings—He wanted me to detach from my security because He wanted to lead me by a new level of faith like Moses. When we built a house with a high mortgage while my first daughter was getting ready for college in six years, you can imagine the reaction from my wife to this word. My darling Jewish wife from Brooklyn had only known financial stability throughout our marriage. She never worried about a bill, a car payment, or a mortgage payment. I arrived home that evening only to learn that she heard the same word independent of me.

At 45 years of age, we took the plunge. We had a brand-new home in a cul-de-sac which was my wife's dream, no savings, and no retirement, and my one daughter was a few years away from college. It seems that God had us right where He wanted us. As Bonnie and I followed the voice of God, supernatural provision was found. "So, what's different here, Lord," I thought. Well, you're about to see what happens!

TWO CITIES

The Lord showed me two cities that constitute two real-time choices every day. The city on my left is everything I don't want it to be, everything God gave to man but he corrupted. It's what it should be, but it's not—a chasing after-the-wind universe, raised up as a modern-day Sodom deeply scarred with hedonism, corruption, and unrighteousness. It's a morning vapor here today, gone tomorrow. My ear and eye gate say, "Do not enter" the world.

The city on the right is everything I want it to be—the way I know it should be, the way it will be. Where small things are great, and everything is pleasing to the eye, lovely and righteous. This is my Father's world of Yeshua's universe. A lost soul is at the corner waiting to be saved, or one is waiting for prayer. Two opposed cities where nothing has changed over two thousand years. Yeshua trained His disciples similarly. He told them, "You are in this world but not of it." This speaks of detachment.

Each morning I turn to the right, putting the other city to my back, giving it my cold shoulder. I *detach*. As the first week led into another, one year into the next. I found myself dancing past the darkness, and no longer letting impermanent things into my soul along with the vicious news cycles and politics. Instead, I submerged my soul in permanence for two years and counting. Although times are troubling, I am absent of worry. Though the times are chaotic, I am unmoved and stationary in my master's universe. I am untouched as one miraculously passing through the Red Sea.

Can you see how these steps can rocket you to a new elevation?

Can you see how God wants this for us?

SIMPLE ADJUSTMENTS

Simple adjustments as these, will vastly increase your spiritual altitude, because each day you're weaving new steps by shifting, adjusting, choosing what is better, and preferring to see better over worse, goodness over meanness. And the most beautiful accomplishment, is being close to everything and nothing affecting yourself. That's strength!

C.S. Lewis said that a continual obsession with looking forward to the eternal world was something that Christians were supposed to do. He wrote: "It is since Christians have largely ceased to think of the other world that they have become so ineffective in this [one]." As mentioned previously, Lewis offered this insightful challenge: "Aim at heaven, you will get earth thrown in. Aim at earth and you get neither." He is describing the art of detachment. To get heavenly, one must detach.

Years ago, I read *The Case Against the Global Economy*. One topic that made an indelible mark on me was over the "cloning of cultures." The author highlighted his research on the devastating effects of the TV when introduced into villages out in the bush. Many women and schoolteachers said they saw an immediate change when television came to the village. Children lost interest in the native language; they wanted only to learn Canadian English. Now the children want new things like cars, yet most communities have no roads. They don't want to learn how to fish on the ice or go hunting anymore. But worst of all, it's what happened to the young and the old relations. Women commented, "TV makes it seem like the young people are all that's important, and the old have nothing to say."[1] Western society is all about self-ego and what we want is the most important.

Research showed that people in the undeveloped world are content with their lives until Western society imposes their values. The same poor but happy people, though more prosperous, are suddenly unhappy. We change their soul to be ego-driven by Western values.

In 1902, Sociologist Charles Horton Cooley wrote: "I am not what I think I am, and I am not what you think I am. I am what I think you think i am."[2]

THE POWER OF EGO

You see, ego is your self-concept of what you believe you need to be whole and happy, and it is always shaped by the world around you—family upbringing and man's expectations of you. Our egos spear through us, stabbing into that tender spot that defines our lives; those things we attach to, why we do the things we do, and the goals that drive us. The same applies to ministry goals. Churches have their egos too. When we're attached to an ego imprinted by someone else's ego, it spears our ability to connect to God's view of our ministry.

What happens when reality doesn't match that image of yourself or your ministry? When your ego-driven attachment causes pain and frustration. When you're unable to reach the personal goals you've set for yourself, you question your abilities and the anointing you carry. Then you can blame others for not meeting your dreams. I say back off slowly from these things to find your true inner self. Discover what God has for you, and you alone. Then from a position of this newfound understanding, you are better equipped to find deeper self-satisfaction, because you're flowing in and through your Father's design.

AN AGE-OLD QUESTION

What we are touching upon is the age-old question of, what is true happiness? Culture tells us that if we obtain all the things we desire or think we are supposed to have, happiness is found. However, the opposite is true.

I learned a long time ago that happiness is not in things, money, position, or fame. Family mattered and how important it was to hang on to the people you loved. I found values in such things as learning, but the right learning. Having space and time to reflect and learn is a sign of vertical living compared to that horizontal living we discussed. How about helping people find meaning, and purpose instead of seeing what we can get from people? How about being makers and creators for each other and, most importantly, God?

ARE YOU READY?

Okay, you're ready to start your first day of Dancing Past the Darkness, and you have no way of knowing what the day will bring or how it will end. You have your schedule, to-do list, and your appointments. You're pretty set on the day. Knowing now that those screaming demands can wait. You'll find that many things can wait. Those moments when you want to know something, but there is no patience to let time reveal it. And how about that harsh word from someone that causes you to walk around with a gaping hole in your day because of a wrong perspective, or what someone said days, months, or weeks ago.

But if you've ever experienced the pain of losing someone, as many have during COVID, there is a colossal shift in scales of importance. This is key to sustaining our *Dancing Past the Darkness*. Detaching and choosing what is better. Paul takes the same idea and turns our head toward God's providence, drawing all creation, even the entire cosmos, toward it. Romans 8:28-39 tells us in part:

> *And we know that in all things, God works for the good of those who love him, who have been called according to his purpose....*

What enables us to detach and trust *is* the certainty and permanence of God. Amidst detachment, I have a picture of an eagle whose flight is unbounded by an open sky—and so is the man who lives detached; his cares have finally been surrendered to the Lord. Yeshua detached often and knew how to say no. He often escaped the busyness of the crowds to renew His strength. Mark 6:31 says:

> *Because so many people were coming and going that they did not even have a chance to eat, he said to [His disciples], "Come with me by yourselves to a quiet place and get some rest."*

Luke 10:38-42 says:

> *Yeshua and his disciples were on their way, he came to a village where a woman named Martha opened her home to him. She had a sister called Mary, who sat at the Lord's feet listening to what he said. But Martha was distracted by all the preparations that had to be made. She came to him and asked, "Lord, don't you care that my sister has left me to do the work by myself? Tell her to help me!" "Martha, Martha," the Lord answered, "you are worried and upset about many things, but few things are needed—or indeed only one. Mary has chosen what is better, and it will not be taken away from her."*

Choose what is better! That's what *Dancing Past the Darkness* did for me. I learned to cooperate with the Lord in a way never experienced before.

Detachment is best portrayed in this prayer by a Monk named Thomas Merton. I can truly relate.

> My Lord God, I have no idea where I am going. I do not see the road ahead of me. I cannot know for certain where it will end. Nor do I know myself, and the fact that I think that I am following your will does not mean that I am doing so. But I believe that the desire to please you does please you. And I hope I have that desire in all I do. I hope that I will never do anything apart from that desire. And I know that you will lead me on the right road as I do this, though I may not know anything about it. Therefore, will I trust you always though I may seem lost and in the shadow of death. I will not fear, for you are ever with me, and you will never leave me to face my perils alone.[3]

STEPS TO TAKE TOWARD DETACHMENT

1. **Soul Cleanse.** Following *Dancing Past the Darkness,* and your 30 Step Devotional, it is strongly recommended to read Heavens Soul Cleanse. It will help launch you into a new spiritual operating system and reboot your soul into heavenly mindedness. When the Soul Cleanse is completed, detachment is more easily accomplished.

2. **Let the Kingdom Consume You:** Practice the tale of two cities: Give the world your cold shoulder and gift the lost your attention and

heart. Choose to detach from the impermanence of things; identify what you have no control over—practice heavenly mindedness.

3. **Be Wide-Eyed:** Notice the beauty of God's handiwork around you. See God through everything instead of the unsaved who see God in nothing. We have another universe that compels us.

4. **Focus On the Moment:** Look for daily opportunities to share God's love. Watch what God does.

5. **You Can't Control Everything:** You have no power over most things, so let it go and don't miss the simple things.

NOTES

1. Jerry Mander, The Case Against the Global Economy (San Francisco: Sierra Club Books, 1997).

2. World of Work Project; https://worldofwork.io/2019/07/who-am-i/; accessed October 27, 2022.

3. Thomas Merton, "A Prayer of Unknowing," Thoughts in Solitude (Farrar, Straus and Giroux, 1999). https://augustinianspirituality.org/2020/11/27/a-prayer-of-unknowing-by-thomas-merton/; accessed October 27, 2022.

6

SAFE HAVEN
MOMENTS

A RECURRENT MESSAGE RUNS THROUGHOUT THIS BOOK: The Glory slows you down. Have you noticed? Yet, from the moment you leave your home, it's like paddling a boat against the wind, right? Remember, *Dancing Past the Darkness* is like dancing atop a fast-moving train. Instead of sipping slowly on that cup of coffee, you chug it down. Once you're on the road, it all begins.

You're sitting at the red light, and not more than a second passes when the light turns green, and a horn honks from behind in "honk language," Move! Get going! Get out of my way! Go faster! That is honk language. It could be one beep with a solid hand—along with a solid beep—or several beeps blasting one after another. It's interesting what you notice when you slow down. By the way, there is no honk language for "Good morning" or "Have a nice day."

Day's events can be disruptive to our soul. A disquieting moment blows in as easy as the wind, bringing increasing dismay at what just occurred. Perhaps it is something you heard. Let's face it, the world is awash with hurt and insult.

It can feel like a corkscrew twisting through you. But always our response at that moment will dictate what's next. Do I remain angry? Do I hold tightly to it even if it feels like burning coal in my chest? I could hold on to my anger or hold on to *Him*.

> Safe haven moments are stops and pauses in a day, remembering that you are just passing through. You're on a sacred pilgrimage.

MY NEW SHANGRI-LA LIFE

The track that we have been on, is getting you excited to launch Dancing Past the Darkness. Perhaps, it will be like sitting in the first row of a Broadway play, and it's your life being played out. If the scene had a name, it would be "My New Shangri-La Life" or "New Epoch" in my life. After all, my promise is that you can live under an open heaven with His Glory every day, and return to Kingdom Normalcy. I say again, you can!

You see, you'll be ready when you have completed this book. You would have learned what it means to give the cold shoulder to the modern-day Sodom world of our time, which is an important key that I have returned from Heaven with. This problem-filled world is not ours, it is theirs. The unsaved, or the carnally minded, are the ones who have no understanding of eternity, and this is their world. Our world and problems are different entirely.

We are not of this world, so we must fan the flame; remain hot for Him; keep our relationship with the Lord intimate; protect and nurture first love works and living. You would have also learned a new angle on seeing not only "who you are" but "what you are." Never again will you let the teaching of man put a yoke of the devil on you—because each day you'll be living with the assurance of His authority and power.

It struck me that everything doesn't need 911 attention, and I don't need to respond to everything—like I need to know, and I need to know now! Sound familiar? A harsh word from someone doesn't need to wring you out. That fire inside that suddenly is ablaze doesn't need to burn because of someone else's lack of self-control. Those demands and responses no longer need to occur when we learn scales of importance—bend the kingdoms of men toward the Kingdom of God. God is looking down to see how we are managing, contending, and moving in and through Him. Can you pause and imagine your life under the watchful eye of your all-loving God.

READY TO DANCE

I can convey the importance of safe haven moments, knowing that they mitigate many daily interruptions. We learn to pause, stop, and allow our soul to retrench with our spiritual side. It's like having an electronic magnetic suspension. There is an expensive option on some cars today that was designed for race cars, electronic magnetic suspension. It is designed to adjust to road conditions, constantly making thousands of adjustments at lightning speed. So fast, in fact, one cannot feel the adjustments being made, except that the car drives much smoother on the road as it is adjusting to bumps, hills, and uneven pavement.

Similarly, we are adjusting each day in real-time, moment to moment, thousands of soul and spiritual adjustments are being made to keep our life stable and smooth. What I am doing is imprinting my soul with this spiritual mapping while building my presence-driven life. Safe haven moments make a mental map of your path through the day, week, and month. Remarkably, it imprints a Glory-driven pattern on your soul as one is stringing these moments together to garner fresh ways forward.

Here are some Safe Haven Moments:

1. **Stop and remember that your true home is not here.** Look up to the heavens regularly to reflect the heavenly Glory created for you. Then reset yourself once again. C.S. Lewis said: "Aim at heaven and you will get earth thrown in. Aim at earth, and you get neither."

2. **Stop and soak up the blessing of His love.** Take a deep breath and hold it for a couple of seconds to appreciate your position as His child. Look up to where your spirit is seated throughout the day (Ephesians 2:6). Half of you is here. The other half is sitting in Glory with Yeshua.

3. **Stop and appreciate His handiwork everywhere you are.** If you are in the countryside or in the middle of the Bronx by the Hudson

River in New York City. Take in these safe haven moments. Pause throughout your day to meditate on His Word, His love for you. Speak with Him, and draw close to Him throughout your day. Listen to people's words so you can learn something in a day. No longer race throughout your day because you want to capture all the opportunities.

INVITE HIS GREATNESS INTO YOUR DAY TODAY

Its early morning, and at first it may sound as if there are only a dozen or more words strung together in bits and pieces. Then a word breaks through, a flow begins, and a string of meditations are forming around your soul. Your voice rises with more, and no more silence around you. Try it! Here is my string of words this morning.

Can you say that I am *Dancing Past the Darkness?*

1. *Learning to Speak the Joy*

As we awaken in the morning, we rise to His glorious throne of justice, whose foundation is of old. He has been the source of all truth, justice, and righteousness from generation to generation. Without Him, no hope exists. With Him, hope radiates through each hour of every day. It's that coin that we carry in our pockets throughout the day. Every impulse thought and action comes under His dominion. He never leaves us or forsakes us. Never is cruelty or insensitivity found in Him; steadfast love and faithfulness meet righteousness.

There is none like You among gods, O Lord. There are no works like Yours. You alone are God. As You are a statute for Israel, a rule for the God of Jacob; You have decreed our lives for eternity. You gave us Your Son, the steadfast and Holy One. Without Him, we would be lost in a deep forest of despair. We would be swept away like a piece of wood carried away by the ocean. You, Lord, have become our hope; only You are the utmost Holy One.

- Is there anything more significant? No!

- Is there anyone more important? No!

- Whose words compare to His, and whose thoughts are more profound? There is no one else like our God.

- Invite His Glory into your day!

- Invite Him into your situation!

- Invite His greatness into your thoughts

- Invite Him to shower you with His rain, and let Heaven dictate your steps today.

Essentially, by taking safe haven moments, you reset yourself again. You're creating life-giving choices that imprint your soul with this spiritual mapping and building a presence-driven life.

2. *Learning to Live in His Glory*

"Show me, Lord, my life's end now that I have seen Your Glory. Let me number my days because all things are fleeting. So it is with life. You have made our days a mere handbreadth, the span of our years we do not know. Everyone is but a breath, even those who seem secure.

A man rushes about, heaping up wealth without knowing whose it will finally be. They chase new causes as the new wind blows in the morning, only to find themselves farther from the light. They tirelessly work to exalt the sons of men, only to be nothing before the Son of Man. You are the fountain of life whose refreshing waters illuminate the darkest soul. In You, there is light, and You are Light! Surely, to live in Your Glory satisfies my soul.

Let my feet be as iron, not easily moved from Your presence.

Let my hands not grow weary or shoulders weakly. Let my eyes not grow faint so I can always see Your Glory. Cause my heart to remain like a young man, that my tongue never stops proclaiming your *truth.*

As the multitudes chase, shadows continue to guide Your people in the path of light. Lord, only You are the fountain of life, and there is light in You alone because You are Light! As the heavens proclaim the Glory of God, let the morning greet us with more of Your enduring promises. Amen.

I pondered the falling snow this morning, marveling at its descent through the air and onto the ground. I have been told that all snowflakes are unique. This is true. They are made differently because each ice crystal has a unique path to the ground. The crystal floats through another cloud of different temperatures and moisture levels causing it to form uniquely. And so it is with every one of us.

When we became living souls by the breath of God, we also became distinct in our unique way. Like the ice crystal, we are formed and shaped by our paths on the ground in our earthly life. We pass through seasons as the crystal passes through different clouds. Our trials, and our unique fiery baptisms form our character and service to our King. No one is the same. Each of us has been given a unique path to proclaim the glory of God in our unique way.

As the skies display His craftsmanship, making Him known day after day, night after night, we speak His Glory without a sound or word. Our voice doesn't need to be heard to display His glory—Live It! It's in our countenance, a warm smile, a gentle hand, a compassionate gaze.

Remember, as the word falls from Heaven today like the rain and the snow, His instructions are perfect, His commandments are right, His commands are clear, giving insight for living. We revere Him, for He alone is pure and lasting forever.

Psalm 19:1-22 (NLT) tells us:

> *The heavens proclaim the glory of God. The skies display his craftsmanship. Day after day they continue to speak; night after night they make him known. They speak without a sound or word; their voice is never heard. Yet their*

message has gone throughout the earth, and their words to all the world.

God has made a home in the heavens for the sun. It bursts forth like a radiant bridegroom after his wedding. It rejoices like a great athlete eager to run the race. The sun rises at one end of the heavens and follows its course to the other end. Nothing can hide from its heat.

The instructions of the Lord are perfect, reviving the soul. The decrees of the Lord are trustworthy, making wise the simple. The commandments of the Lord are right, bringing joy to the heart. The commands of the Lord are clear, giving insight for living. Reverence for the Lord is pure, lasting forever. The laws of the Lord are true; each one is fair.

They are more desirable than gold, even the finest gold. They are sweeter than honey, even honey dripping from the comb. They are a warning to your servant, a great reward for those who obey them.

7

LEARN THE WAY OF GLORY

I WAS DANCING TOWARD THE END OF THE PREVIOUS CHAPter; I'm wondering if you noticed. You see, as the glory was spilling out of me, I was alone in the deep shadow of something, not knowing where to go next. That's the way it was upon my return as I was learning the way of Glory. Time flew by quicker than I have ever experienced. I was delirious with Him—I wanted to possess more of Him—and He me it seems. But I also felt I was like floating on a piece of driftwood to cling to. The familiar choppy waters of the world were too harsh in the beginning.

I am often asked, can one live in the Glory daily? I'll respond with a very Jewish response. You know, with another question! Can we live one half seated in heavenly places, the other in the mortal earthly realms? The Bible says yes. We were created for it, and our Lord rose for it, and the Spirit inhabited our lives for it. So yes, one can live a Glory-driven life amid our tumultuous world.

You see, the glory causes us to perk toward rightness and order. It's how the Glory animates our soul toward putting things in their proper places. It compels us to put our house back in order. Former ways of thinking appear as if they had just come out of a deep forest, and adjustments need to be made. God was dropping little bits of information about how things would be. Everything was preparing me for *Dancing Past the Darkness*.

> ## FOR THIS REASON, THE GLORY HAS A WAY OF LOCKING YOU INTO SELF-INSPECTION AND REFLECTION ON THE WORLD AROUND YOU.

The Glory will animate your soul and body, so whether you eat or drink or whatever you do, all things are done for the Glory of God (1 Corinthians 10:31). God's Glory is seen in His love, longsuffering, and forgiveness—it's also seen in how you live. His character, for instance, is the quintessence of Glory, as is His presence. The Glory is the manifestation of His Spirit and the indicator of His presence. The Glory in you is how people see God.

> *The Lord, the God of gods, has spoken and summoned the earth from the rising of the sun to its setting. From Zion, perfect in beauty, God shines forth* (Psalm 50:1-2 NCB).
>
> *He said to Me, "You are My Servant, Israel, in whom I will show My glory"* (Isaiah 49:3 NASB).
>
> *For God, who said, "Light shall shine out of darkness," is the One who has shone in our hearts to*

give the Light of the knowledge of the glory of God
in the face of Christ (2 Corinthians 4:6 NASB).

If the Spirit is the wind, or *Ruach,* the Glory is what makes God's presence known. The Spirit is invisible, but it is working and active to produce the Glory that God would be revealed in you. Living in and through the Glory then, manifests a greater show of God. One can say that the Glory connotes a habitation rather than a visitation, so the glory reveals, defines, and expresses His presence. The closer we come to Him, we begin to experience more of His Glory. But when the Spirit is quenched and grieved through sin, the Glory lifts like a cloud, because it is as light as a feather in the face of sin. But it is so heavy when it is present it can push you to the floor.

DIFFERENT GLORIES

God manifests Himself in many glories. There is an earthly glory and heavenly Glory. "There are also heavenly bodies, and there are earthly bodies; but the splendor of the heavenly bodies is one kind, and the splendor of the earthly bodies is another" (1 Corinthians 15:40). Heaven and its Glory defy the imagination.

There is the splendor of heavenly bodies to one degree and the grandeur of the earthly bodies. These glories have been stationed in everyday life from the day of creation. Romans 1:20 (Amplified) states:

> *For ever since the creation of the world His invis-*
> *ible attributes, His eternal power, and divine*

nature, have been clearly seen, being understood through His workmanship [all His creation, the wonderful things that He has made], so that they [who fail to believe and trust in Him] are without excuse and defense.

So yes, it's there for the unsaved and the saved alike. It should remind the unsaved that God's handprint is everywhere, and that He exists.

Miraculously, there is a glory that we carry in these mortal bodies. His Spirit is a glory, and the Lord is that Spirit of Glory. This God of Glory governs the world. There is a Celestial Glory and Kingdom (the highest, most noble of the degrees of Glory) where God reigns. There is the Terrestrial realm as terrestrial bodies and celestial bodies, all differ in Glory as the moon differs from the sun (1 Corinthians 15:40). *"It is the glory of God to conceal a matter, but the glory of kings to search out a matter"* (Proverbs 25:2 NKJV).

Go ahead, go out every morning like a king and search them out. King David often went out to take the time to gaze upward into a boundless expanse of Glory.[1] David saw it as a privilege to study the stars, scan the skies, and read creation like a book of our Creator. All are telling of the Glory of God you see, and any part of creation has more instruction than any human mind can give.

Did you catch the Glory fever yet?

Beloved, I see it this way. One cannot descend a hill and cross far over a broad spanned steel bridge, or a raging river to break free from His desire to manifest His Glory in your life. You cannot escape what He wants for you. You see, if I can get you to catch the Glory fever, your focus on earthly things becomes smaller, and more room is made for Kingdom Normalcy in your life, thereby revealing more Glory and more of Him.

Did you catch the Glory fever yet?

GLORY AND POWER

The Glory is also measured in His power. Who regulates the forces of nature, science, physics, and medicine? God. He can choose to defy the most intelligent scientists and drown them in complete puzzlement. He has rulership of the wind. He commands the wind to rise from the ground or descend from the Heavens and blow in God's chosen direction. The rains can fall at His choosing, or He holds them in His heavenly aquifers. The tiniest creature will stand up at His command, as will the ice, rain, snow, tempest, airways, sub terrains, currents, underground streams, rivers and lakes, and the walls of the mightiest oceans. Its all the way of the glory, and the power of our Creator. It's the way of Heaven.

There is no power greater, every other power is lesser. God's Glory would not be silent or still if we stood in place motionless, or the wind sat still on the ground, and every bird and creature was frozen in time. God's Glory is the first thing planted in us when we come to faith, the first thing people see in and through us, and it greets us when we cross over and walk through the literal pearly gates. As an NDE (Near Death Encounter) or ALS (After Life Survivor), Heaven remains a consuming fire as does His Glory. Although I am on earth, my obsession is for the Glory to define me so that others find the King of Glory.

GOING BEYOND THE VEIL

You see, my arrival in Heaven was not met with subtlety, I was beyond the veil of the mortal realm. The finest tenor couldn't sing adequately enough to communicate its essence; the finest artist is left ill-equipped, because they don't have paints for the colors or the strokes to capture it. Heaven is the city adorned like a bride prepared for her Groom on their wedding night. Heaven was waiting for me!

Did you catch that?

I was prostrate before the throne, as I saw the Lord high and lifted, drowning me in fearful, reverent awe. There was a train of His glory that filled every corner of Heaven. I saw the outline of the Lord's feet, and His hands resting upon the throne. I recall the strength in His hands. He sat upon the throne as the resurrected triumphant One who subjugated the devil, making the way possible for me to be there. God sent His Son for sinners like me, and now I am prostrate before the highest cosmos, the purest, most eternal power.

Back on earth, days draw to a quiet breath in a simpler life, quitting in near-perfect silence, at times breakable only by my breathing, as I am recovering and maintaining the ebb and flow of the glory mindset. Once you start, you'll begin to recall the enigmatic power of God. Go ahead, pause here, visualize the immense greatness of God and hold on it. I call this the *heavenly jump exercise:* Jumping out of the temporal and into the spiritual.

Try this jump exercise!

Visualize the pillar of fire that descended from Heaven in the night sky as the Israelites traveled through the wilderness. Then, visualize the cloud accompanying them day after day.

Draw near to the fire on the altar of Mount Moriah as Abraham brought Isaac to be sacrificed. I have imagined this situation: The fire is hot and ready, and perhaps a slight wind is blowing, causing the flames to flicker and dance, cracking, popping, and sending sparks into the air. Perhaps dumbstruck, Abraham clutches a large knife ready to make contact with his son's throat, his only son, Isaac. What was in his mind? One can only imagine. Every second loomed large with suspense. I can only foresee Abraham's pulse like a machine gun firing inside his chest.

Then move your mind's eye over to the Red Sea, as it is splitting in two, making a dry path for the Israelites to pass through. I see every Israelite moving with a steadying hand on the back of the other, carefully, and quietly, while the children fearfully stay in step, perhaps, whispering over the shoulder's, "Stay steady! Look forward! Push! Hurry! Pharaoh's mighty army is on our heels!"

I see the last Israelites place their feet on the other side when there is a momentary pause. Then, everyone hears a strange roar as the sea is folding back, and just like a giant Leviathan, it opens its mouth and swallows Pharaoh's mighty army. Pharaoh is sitting on the other side in utter shock. His army, empire, his firstborn son, everything is gone. But in another scene, I admit my dismay too. I visualize the death of my Messiah—I don't want to see it. Then jubilation sweeps over me at the empty tomb—followed by thoughts of Pentecost in the Upper Room.

There is an important point here that I want to introduce you to. Our lives are like a stone vault filled with heavenly, miraculous memories. They may not be as grand as the ones mentioned, but yours are extraordinary and miraculous. They are like your personal glory arrows that you can shoot into the night sky, releasing your own memories of His glory and faithfulness. Enter your vault, sit, and shoot your arrows into the night sky. Recall your memories. I am sure there are too many Glories to count.

NOTE

1. Charles H. Spurgeon, *Treasury of David* (Carol Stream, IL: Hendrickson Publishers/Tyndale House, 1988).

8

LEARN THE GLORY MINDSET

I'M SLOUCHED DOWN A BIT NOW AS I HAVE BEEN WRITING since 3 a.m., and it is now 11 a.m. One of the costs of a holy obsession, is that there is no rest day and night. Hopefully, you have that enthusiasm—that vigorous, cheerful offering for Him too. We're getting ready to run without looking back. The spirit is activated, and we are participating. The glory mindset will change you.

Surely, it was big, that change that followed the glory side, and I knew it. God knew it. Everyone who knew me knew it. COVID however, provided a strange shelter for two years as a shield against the harsh realities of this new life. There I was standing whenever I could, throwing myself into His arms, trying to make sense of it all. Privileged to return, the blessing of the glory, yet the awkwardness of adjusting back. But I never got back onto that fast-moving train, and now I am trying to get you off. We've all been wondering how we can stop it or change the course of our days. I was changed from the inside out and found the Glory mindset.

When I was in the Great Hall of Heaven, I wanted to run on the streets of gold, as my boyhood youth and vigor were back. When one crosses over, you have already changed out of your mortal-like costumes and come to the grace of a Holy audience of One. I remind myself that I belong to this place, as it belongs to you. It's in your bloodline. In Heaven, every column and surface seemed to be covered in gold with a fierce fiery glow. As I saw majestic mountains ascending the iridescent blueish canopy, I saw luscious hills green, vibrant, and living. I saw a river, as waterfalls were making their presence known cascading down gracefully, and majestically. God's presence was everywhere as One who sets a calming hand on your shoulder, and you are struck by His glory, majesty, love, and warmth.

In addition to being the perfect, Holy Place, an unwavering admiration and worship is being directed by the ideal director, the Holy One, who is gently guiding all of Heaven in holy admiration. I was savoring every moment. Every moment was like one drop of rain that could nourish the earth.

What I desire for your pursuit of a glory mindset, requires intention with a heart of desperation. In Heaven, it's easy because everything is supernaturally queued for Glory. On earth, it takes effort, desire, and discipline.

LOOKING DOWN FROM HEAVEN

Let me say that the world/earth is fascinating too. Earthly life doesn't need to be boring, it can be Glory filled. It's all what you choose to see, and what you don't see. What is the focus of your attention on any day?

For instance, small things are great just as great things have greatness. Sure, the ant is not a symbol of lion-like power and prowess, but it is no less miraculous as the sea's great Leviathan. One drop of rain is no less miraculous than a single snowflake, a mighty tempest, a gentle breeze. It all varies on our perspective, and the subject of our focus. If our lids turn upward, we will see the beauty in great things and small things. It's one of the ways to feed the Glory mindset.

In Job 12:7-10 for instance, we are spurred on to have these inquiring minds. It tells us to:

> *Ask the animals, and they will teach you, or the birds in the sky, and they will tell you; or speak to the earth, and it will teach you, or let the fish in the sea inform you. Which of these does not know that the hand of the LORD has done this? For in his hand is the life of every creature and the breath of all mankind.*
>
> *In his hand are the depths of the earth, and the mountain peaks belong to him. The sea is his, for he made it, and his hands formed the dry land* (Psalm 95:4-5).

These simple acts cultivate the Glory mindset in us.

Watch something happen when the Spirit activates you for the Glory. The Spirit begins to animate your soul so that *"whether you eat or drink or whatever you do, you do it all for the glory of God"* (1 Corinthians 10:31). You come into a Glory mindset. The Bible reminds us that there are many glories to occupy our holy *curiosity.*

I SEE SOMETHING ELSE

Now let us turn ever so slightly while holding onto the Glory chorus that has been heard throughout this work. In the illumination of the Glory, shadows jump out everywhere. Every morning I go to the corner bagel store for my tea, only to see the same older men talking about the weather and congratulating each other on various perceived accomplishments. I see people entirely unaware of the times and the hour we live in. God's people share the same disease.

They, too, speaking of God's people, are scurrying to and fro, uptight, racing to the red light. No sooner than the light turns green, a horn blasts to move. Why has it only been a second. Perhaps the speed of a twinkling of an eye. As believers, we cannot be driven by the cultural stopwatch. The Glory and presence abhor it. Make no mistake, a harried life for God's people is destructive. It's one of the reasons I no longer wear a watch. I wear a compass on my wrist, always reminding me that position is more important than time. This harried culture pulls down upon the soul, keeping you so occupied and distracted so that there isn't enough room for the Glory to move, because you are shoulder to shoulder with the world's activities.

As previously noted, the Bible places a high value on rest and peaceful living. Even Yeshua escaped the busyness of the crowds to renew His strength many times. Mark 6:31 says, *"Because so many people were coming and going that they did not even have a chance to eat, he said to* [His disciples], *'Come with me by yourselves to a quiet place and get some rest.'"*

I remember when New York City was a ghost town during the COVID lockdown. People were home with loved ones. Neighborhoods were filled with people talking to each other. Family walks were ordinary. Everyone was discovering things that they had never noticed.

Dallas Willard said, "Among the practices that can help us attend to soul care at a basic level are *solitude* and *silence*. We practice these by finding ways to be alone and away from talk and noise. We rest, observe, and stop 'smell the roses'— dare we say it?—we do *nothing*! God can use this discipline as a means of grace. We may even find another reminder of grace—that we are saved, justified by His redeeming power—not by our strivings and achievements."

I hope my words have pulled on that deep thread. I see someone reading this, perhaps pausing to clear their throat as sighs are heard, "Tell me more." You see, there is something in all of us of an eternal nature, we are imbued with it, and we need to understand more. So, hang on as we descend deeper!

GLORY MINDSET

Now if you haven't caught my subtleties, one prerequisite for Dancing Past the Darkness: You must notice the beauty most people miss. IT'S THE WAY! And if you can become a holy admirer, YOU WILL SEE THE BEAUTY IN YOUR DAY. Go beyond yourself—and get outside your daily world consciousness and pressures—get into a Heavenly consciousness—a Glory mindset!

For instance, most people hub around the darker happenings of daily life, the Glory mindset sees the beauty in a day and the blessings that fill it. Try to put a Kingdom-oriented spin on everything. When others see doom and gloom, fix your eyes on a discouraged soul and look to be God's hand extended; experience the sick healed or a word of compassion to a needy soul. Step out of yourself and your schedule and pray for someone in your day. Incorporate *stops* in your day to tell someone that God loves them and that He has not forgotten them.

SEEING DIFFERENTLY

I know you might be wondering if it is possible to live this way; slowing down, praying for people, enjoying God's creation, having inquiring minds, and searching eyes like an explorer. Once again from Proverbs 25:2 (NLT) says, *"It is God's privilege to conceal things and the king's privilege to discover them."* So, go on a discovery. Be an adventurer!

If we slow down, and get into a Glory mindset, we discover a kaleidoscope of treasures to be wide-eyed about. Start with the Bible which is also "The" book of nature revealing three leaves, Heaven, earth, and sea. Heaven is the first and the most glorious; and by its creation, we can see the beauties of the other two. Cloudy days remind you of the Glory that comes on the clouds. Look it up in Scripture. It's there! Rainy days remind me of the water being discharged from Heaven to water the seed of the ground that there is bread for the eater—it is like His word that doesn't return void. Nature needs a drink. You'll find it in the Bible! Let your days greet you with eyes wide open to opportunities to *see* a lost soul come into the Kingdom.

Dare to be different. Slow down to hear and listen more. Every day Yeshua read people like a book to engage them for the Kingdom. He read a rich man's thoughts who thought it was easy to follow Him. Today, its easy to meet someone visibly hardened by life with no apparent faith in their eyes, yet you can feel compassion for them.

> **Learn to boost the good and reframe your thoughts by building awareness of the present so the spirit's voice grows stronger.**

The Bible calls the heavens plural for their variety, existing of the watery heavens with the solar heavens, and all the day's glories, like the starry heavens with all their marvels of the night. Any part of creation has more instruction than the human mind will ever exhaust. No matter which way you turn, it is like a giant glorious jigsaw puzzle.

Before I end this chapter, I want to speak to the naysayers around every corner who are pushing impatiently, ready to tell you, "You cannot live this way in the presence and under the Glory." They are a product of the culture. What slips into the crowd of our Christian culture lay the notion that our toilsome trek through life is one's lot pending Heaven. Notice the two words: *trek* and *toilsome*. I prefer *dance* and *pleasure*. The naysayers are dead wrong. You can pull Heaven down daily, notwithstanding those pundits, traditionalists, and conventionalists. I hope my words offered some enticement to come closer, so you are not pensive. A lot happens around here that will surprise you.

CONCLUSION

Friend, life's bruising that sin brings can only be healed at the feet of Yeshua who hung on that crossbeam for you. The blood on the crossbeam proves today, two thousand years later, how I got to Heaven. Instantly His death opened the door to our eternal destiny.

Give your life to the Lord today, and don't miss out on the most glorious place created for you, Heaven. In Heaven, there is no worry about anything. The order of things is pure, right, straight, and untouched by human hands. The glory is bright and blinding, yet it penetrates the atmosphere with a sweet rose fragrance. Did you ever think we should live more of our lives marked by a deeper heavenly mindset, and His presence in the here and now? The answer is yes! He loves sinners and cares for every soul.

Pray this prayer:

> *Lord, come into my life and be Lord of my life. Forgive me for my sin and thank You for sending Your Son to die. I receive my Messiah, the Lamb of God who died for me. Fill me with Your Spirit and make me a new creation.*

9

LIVING IN GLORY AUTHORITY

WHAT HAPPENS WHEN GLORY MARRIES KNOWLEDGE?

Did you ever dream about being a princess or a prince? They have it all, don't they? Beautiful clothing, grand castles, fame, fortune, a wonderland few will ever experience. That's why I love Ephesians 2:6. It's the place where glory and authority originate. It's such an important passage for our life of Dancing Past the Darkness.

C.S. Lewis termed us "little Christs" and a "good infection," he says. Paul uses the Greek tense for seated, something that occurred in the past, and it remains true when writing. We will not be established with Yeshua in Heaven when He returns; we have been seated with Him at salvation and are still there since then.

The word "places" carries the same idea as spheres or realms.

I noted in the Introduction that we are warrior brides on the one, living in the glory on the other. Though it may seem contradictory, it is an accurate depiction of a Glory-centered life. In John 12:31 (NKJV), we're told that Satan is the "ruler of this world," which indicates a realm and region. Then in Daniel 10:13,20 (NKJV), we see this reference to the *"prince of the king-dom of Persia."* This dark prince opposes the powerful Glory angel Gabriel, and the even mightier Glory prince Michael.

In Matthew 4, Satan comes to Yeshua and offers Him what is His anyway, the kingdoms of the world. But through the cross, Yeshua took back the authority forfeited in Adam (Colossians 2:14-15). So in Matthew 28:18, Yeshua states that all authority has been given to Him, and then to us. This is what some call Kingdom Authority, what I call Glory Authority. As noted in the Introduction, *Dancing Past the Darkness* requires the right knowledge.

> Proverbs 18:15 (ESV): *"An intelligent heart acquires knowledge, and the ear of the wise seeks knowledge."*
>
> Proverbs 2:10 (ESV): *"For wisdom will come into your heart, and knowledge will be pleasant to your soul."*
>
> 1 Corinthians 12:8 (ESV): *"For to one is given through the Spirit the utterance of wisdom, and to another, the utterance of knowledge according to the same Spirit."*

The Glory cannot operate in the wrong knowledge, as when one believes the day of miracles has ended with the apostles, or that sickness is God's will. Or that God doesn't heal anymore because we are in a different dispensation. When church leaders openly attribute many of their problems to the devil, it's like a stream of dark informants stealing away the authority from God's people. It's like the enemy constantly raising its flag in the House of God. This feverish hammering is impertinent as leaders. I see the devil mounting gunports in the House of God, shooting the people of God in their own house.

Today, many do not believe in the Baptism in the Holy Ghost, signs and wonders, and gifts of *dunamis* power. Many believe that born-again believers can be demons possessed, and Satan and his demons can oppress them and be the cause and effect of every problem. This is a gross annihilation of power, Biblically incorrect, and highly offensive to the name of Yeshua. The early apostles and the church never believed these things.

Yeshua was always bringing the right instruction to His disciples so they walk in this Glory Authority. They watched when Yeshua fought the devil, as the Glory still surrounded Him.

When Yeshua taught the Pharisees in Matthew 12 about demons, the Glory was present. When He gave such specifics about casting out the strong man in the same chapter, the Glory was present. The Glory produces authority and constrains the devil when proper understanding is present. As Jesus cast out an unclean spirit in Mark 1:23-28, everyone was amazed; not only did He operate in and through the Glory, He knew who the demons were and how to excise them.

In Acts 19:15, the seven sons of Sceva, a Jewish chief priest, tried to mimic casting out demons, but they had no knowledge of Yeshua and the Glory of His power. It didn't take very long for the demons to answer them because they had more knowledge than the sons of Sceva: *"Jesus I know, and Paul I know, but who are you?"* Then the man with the evil spirit jumped on them and overpowered them.

Another time there was a great haul of fish (Luke 5:1-11), but Peter first fished on the wrong side. The King of Glory showed him the rights side! On another day, Yeshua and some disciples got into a boat, and His disciples followed Him. Suddenly a furious storm came up on the lake when the waves swept over the boat. Jesus was sleeping. The disciples woke Him, saying, "Lord, save us! We're going to drown!" He replied, "You of little faith, why are you so afraid?" Then He got up and rebuked the winds and the waves, and it was completely calm. The men were amazed and asked, "What kind of man is this? Even the winds and the waves obey him!" They needed to learn something. Peter needed to learn something when Yeshua said to him, "Satan get behind me." We need to learn some things here.

YESHUA WAS THE CONSUMMATE GLORY MAN

Friend, right knowledge is the vessel that allows the Glory to flow. In Colossians 2:14-15 we read of Yeshua:

> *having canceled the charge of our legal indebtedness, which stood against us and condemned us; he has taken it away, nailing it to the cross. And having disarmed the powers and authorities, he*

*made a public spectacle of them, triumphing over
them by the cross.*

We learn from this passage that Yeshua disarmed Satan
and his demons at the cross, because Satan could not find any
cause for accusation against Him. Hence, dark rulers, author-
ities, and principalities were openly disgraced as Yeshua rose
in triumph. Yet countless believers arm Satan against themselves by wrong teaching and messaging in church culture. If
our sin record is erased by Yeshua's sacrifice, how can there
be accusation? Colossians makes this quite clear.

THIRD HEAVEN POSITION

I saw this verse in a new light and knowledge: "And hath
raised us up together, and made us sit together in heavenly
places in Yeshua" (Ephesians 2:6 KJV). When our Messiah
conquered the spiritual realms, His experience became our
spiritual experience by making us into a new creation. Our
spirit followed accordingly in the path upward, just as He
went to sit at the Father's right hand.

Yes, you are on earth. But you are also "spiritually" seated
in Heaven with Yeshua, the very place of power and authority. This position was the result of one Man who competed
for supremacy and won. As He steadied Himself on the
slopes of the Mount of Olives fixed on the cross, He would
raise us up with Him, seating us with Him in the heavenly
realm, "spiritually" speaking. The roots of this world tore
away, so that our roots would forever be entwined in the
heavenly realms.

Take note.

First, *"heavenly places"* describe the spiritual status of our spirits that govern our lives on earth. Seated in the heavenly places makes dancing past the darkness possible. We have been given 3rd heaven authority over 2nd and 1st heaven principalities.

Second, an identity transplant also took place that is analogous to a medical heart transplant—the work of Yeshua replaced us in our old selves. So it is with us today—we became a new spiritual creation residing in and through our material body like Yeshua; one part on earth, and the other sitting in Heaven. As in the first Adam, all have died, leading the whole human race to death. Everyone is made alive in the Second Adam, Yeshua. First Corinthians 15:45 (NKJV) states, *"The last Adam became a life-giving spirit."* And it is here in this "life-giving" Spirit we share in the life of Yeshua seated with Him in heavenly places (Ephesians 2:6).

Although there is an outwardly wasting away of our physical bodies, we are inwardly being renewed day by day by the Spirit of Yeshua. *"Since you have been raised with Yeshua, set your heart on things above. Set your minds on things above, not earthly things"* (Colossians 3:1-2). In other words, set your soul on things above and align itself with your spirit.

As we are part of this first fruits of the Resurrection with the Lord—Yeshua in Body, Soul, and Spirit, we in Spirit—we will become the ultimately exalted, spiritually resurrected sons and daughters of God, always empowering life in the present, always communicating Spirit to spirit. God seated us with Him in the heavenly realms (see Ephesians 1:3,20; 2:6; 3:10; 6:12).

- Whereas Yeshua had died physically (Eph. 1:20), unbelievers were dead spiritually (Eph. 2:1-3).

- While Yeshua was raised physically (Eph. 1:20), unbelievers are made alive and grow with Him spiritually (Eph. 2:5-6).

As we are present on the material earth, God imprints His will and presence in our souls and spirit. Through our bodies, we're animating our communion with Him. The Word is in plain sight: God raised you up with Yeshua and seated you in the heavenly realms. This means you can live above your circumstances because you come from a place of victory.

I am sure you were pricked a bit when you started across this field of thought. I get it! It is like something that appeared behind a tree as we walked together, then disappeared. You say, "Wait a minute, what was that?" Something just happened. And there it is again.

SCRIPTURES TO REVIEW

1. **Romans 8:15-17 (NASB):** *For you have not received a spirit of slavery leading to fear again, but you have received a spirit of adoption as sons and daughters by which we cry out, "Abba! Father!" The Spirit Himself testifies with our spirit that we are children of God, and if children, heirs also, heirs of God and fellow heirs with Christ, if indeed we suffer with Him so that we may also be glorified with Him.*

2. **Romans 8:23** (ESV): *And not only the creation, but we ourselves, who have the first fruits of the Spirit, groan inwardly as we wait eagerly for adoption as sons, the redemption of our bodies.*

3. **2 Corinthians 5:5** (ESV): *He who has prepared us for this very thing is God, who has given us the Spirit as a guarantee.*

4. **2 Corinthians 1:22** (ESV): *And who has also put his seal on us and given us his Spirit in our hearts as a guarantee.*

10

MYSTERIES REVEALED

WHAT I LEARNED ABOUT SPIRITUAL WARFARE

Let us take another perspective, and let wisdom guide us. In quantum physics, there is a term called "entanglement": When two items pass through the same source, they vibrate with the same frequency until one touches another.

Similarly, we have been entangled with Yeshua through the Holy Spirit, made possible only by His sacrifice for us. Our spirit vibrates with Heaven's frequency when believers fellowship with one another. We might not be cognizant of it, but there is a metaphysical aspect of our lives that is part of our new creation. Although our soul and body are on earth, our spirit is in heavenly places, as stated previously. The state of the Spirit then is to be lived in the body much like Yeshua's time on earth, though He was without sin, and we are not. This is nothing less than miraculous—Spirit to spirit—soul to spirit—body to soul.

Friend, Yeshua's post-resurrection state was a new creation in His day (Philippians 3:20). These words may feel like you just stepped into quicksand, but I couldn't escape it. When my yes snapped open from this conversation between my spirit and the Lord, I leaned back into God's Word in Ephesians 2:6, that we discussed, and a C-Change event occurred in me. We, His children, are living earthly yet already spiritually resurrected. (See John 11:25; Colossians 1:18; Romans 8:11; 1 Corinthians 15:35-37, 42, 52-53.)

MORE MYSTERY REVEALED

One afternoon I experienced the other side of the Glory, the darkness, when God invited me into the Second Heaven where demons reside. I guess I needed a new knowledge.

I was standing upon a firmament separating the Second Heaven, or the lower from the upper airways, demons could not cross or access me. I saw first-hand how demons have no supremacy where the people of God inhabit. They hate the Glory so much because the Glory suffocates them like the name of Jesus dries up cancer cells. I stared at the demon as he was trying to rise over the catacomb-like structure, never losing interest in attacking me. Thinking back, I cringe at the way he looked, and how pitifully weak the demon was.

But once again, the conventional glass would be shattered for me into a thousand pieces, and my long-held theology would be turned on its head. One demon (and I noticed hordes) desperately tried reaching up and taking hold of my ankles. Pitifully and powerlessly, its futile attempts frustrated him even more. I can only imagine the devil's frustration because he is a hardened privateer when he knows he cannot touch the people of God.

Paul's letters come to mind, reminding me of what I have always known but never witnessed before in such a way. He says unbelievers are caught in the devil's snares (2 Timothy 2:26). In another area, he states, *"In their case the god of this world has blinded the minds of the* unbelievers, *to keep them from seeing the light of the gospel of the glory of Christ, who is the image of God"* (2 Corinthians 4:4 ESV).

Then these words: *"In which you once walked, following the course of this world, following the prince of the power of the air, the spirit that is now at work in the* sons of disobedience" (Ephesians 2:2 ESV).

You see, we, the redeemed, the "sons of obedience," are no longer under the rule or influence of Satan or his demonic horde. Colossians 1:13-14 (ESV) states, "He has delivered us from the domain of darkness and transferred us to the kingdom of his beloved Son, in whom we have redemption, the forgiveness of sins." We are not waiting to be transferred; we have been transferred to the Kingdom of His Son.

DOMAIN OF DARKNESS

The devil's domain of darkness consists of the shadow of death, hell, and the whole sphere of Satan on earth as the prince and power of the air. His demons and dark inspiration can break through the first heaven into the lives of mortal men. The Bible indicates that our adversary is the god of this world, but it does not mean that he was given ultimate authority. No! Rather, he rules over the unbelieving world specifically.

Even though Satan is the prince and the power of the air (Ephesians 2:2) and ruler of the world (John 12:31), he moves and reigns in the first heaven for unbelievers, and remains in the lower air ways below our feet for believers. The blood of Yeshua puts a blood border around us that cannot be crossed by the devil or his demon army.

> Yet at the cost of the glory in people's lives, I suspect that these so-called demons are running their imaginary raiding campaigns because of people's preoccupation with demons and demonology.

The above statement fits my suspicion over the course of ministry, which is explained further in the next chapter. We, beloved, are the people of the "breakthrough" because Yeshua broke through the dark realm rendering the blood all-powerful and victorious. Genesis 3:14 says, *"The Lord God said to the serpent, "Because you have done this, cursed are you above all livestock and all wild animals! You will crawl on your belly and you will eat dust all the days of your life."*

TWO THEATERS OF CONFLICT

Given the above comments, more must be said about demons. These enemies of the glory. I noted earlier in this work that Kingdom power and living is an amalgam of Glory and authority. This authority comes with knowledge; an inherent awareness of the spirit power that unbelievers do not possess. As we possess spiritual power, we are better equipped to know our enemy because our enemy knows us (Acts 19:15), and we can hold the front as the warring bride living in and through the Glory. In the next chapter we will drill deeper into my thesis that states, we have turned soul problems into devil problems. But we first need a reminder of what happened when the Messiah came two thousand years ago and the environment in His day.

There are two theaters of conflict that we face. The first is the soul, our inner being. The second is the outside world, where the prince and power of the air rules (Ephesians 2:2).

But how do we navigate these two?

First, demons are fallen angels who lost their physical and spiritual attributes when God first created them. There are demonic hordes of these fallen angels (2 Peter 2:4,6; Luke 7:21; 8:2), and some are worse and more powerful than other's (Matthew 12:43,45; Mark 9:17-29). Following their fall, they began to decay. Like their master, they are in a spirit of delusion, and they are pathetic because they have no power over us, yet they try.

The word "demon" is used in the Gospels close to 50 times and is always in the context of unbelievers. The same is true of the word "devil," used 30 times. It is essential to know that there is no account of a believer in Yeshua being demon-possessed in the New Testament. All the accounts take place in unbelievers. In Yeshua's day, demons and demon possession were part of the fabric of Judaea Hellenic life. Demons had free reign to suppress and possess people and animals at will (Luke 11:24-25; Mark 5:13). It was like the "Wild West" for demons because there was no authority to bind the strong man before Yeshua came, so demons roamed freely.

Demons dwelt in desolate regions, in the mountains, among the tombs, and in dry, waterless places (Mark 5:2,5; Luke 11:24). They had great freedom due to widespread idolatry, licentiousness, polytheism, witchcraft, sorcery, sexual immorality, impurity, and debauchery (Galatians 5:20). They possessed men, women, boys, and girls (Matthew 4:24; Luke 8:2, 9:38-39; Mark 7:25).

Demons in Yeshua's day caused some to be dumb (unable to speak); they caused blindness; inability to hear; to be savage; to possess superhuman strength and appear insane (Matthew 8:28; 9:32-33; 12:22; Mark 5:2-5; 9:25). They spoke through the mouth of the one whom they possessed, as the demoniac (Luke 4:33-36), they knew Yeshua as the Son of God, but they also knew their destiny (Mark 5:7; Matthew 8:29). So commonplace were roving demons that Jewish exorcists traveled to different towns to perform exorcisms on children and adults (Matthew 12; Acts 19:11-17; 19:13). Of course, because their power was counterfeit, and no one had the authority to bind the strong man, the individual received only short-term relief (Mark 1:7; 3:22-30).

This unprecedented time would come to serve and authenticate Yeshua's Messiahship (Matthew 12; Mark 5:1-20; Luke 10:18). You see, everything would change when Yeshua binds the strong man (Matthew 12). A new dispensation of authority was about to begin.

A NEW SHERIFF IN TOWN

As the rule of the Kingdom over darkness was set in motion at the ministry of Yeshua, it would be immediate and progressive, culminating at a future time of the Millennial Reign of Messiah. As the Old Testament repeatedly reminds us, and as Yeshua affirmed in Luke 10:18, on that day, the defeat of the prince and power of the air will be swift and final.

The Kingdom's announcement would become the only new ruling authority from that time forward. This is consistent with what Luke writes in the next chapter (11:14-23), where he identifies Yeshua, who binds the strong man, Satan. Having secured the strong man (Satan), Yeshua and His disciples can plunder Satan's realm. This holds true for us today. In fact, we plunder Satan's kingdom the moment we become saved and blood-washed. Nothing has changed, beloved. This fits with what Yeshua said after His statement about Satan (Luke 10:19-20), where He grants the disciples power over the forces of evil.

THE SEVENTY-TWO ARE SENT OUT

In Matthew 10:17-20, seventy-two disciples were sent to heal the sick and free the captives. They returned excited that even the demons had submitted to them in Yeshua's name. New power and authority, formerly unknown, were not seen before the Messiah came. Yeshua acknowledged their excitement, saying, "I saw Satan fall like lightning from heaven." He is not telling us Satan instantly fell from Heaven as He talked to the seventy men. Yeshua explains that Satan's power had been broken, and it was collapsing before their eyes. Henceforth, the demons and the devil would be subject to Yeshua's authority.

The seventy-two disciples had cast out the devils because the demons respected their power and the name of Yeshua over evil spirits. From that point on, Satan's power would decline, contracting in proportion to the rising power of the Kingdom. The seventy witnessed nothing less than the reversal of the effects of sin and death through the devil's deception in Genesis 3.

Consequently, Yeshua would inaugurate a new dispensation of power and authority. He defeated Satan's power by His blood and resurrection; never again could a child of God be demon-possessed. The relative comments by commentator Albert Barnes on Colossians 2:15 (NKJV) *("And having spoiled principalities and powers, He made a public spectacle of them openly, triumphing over them in it"):*

- 1 John 4:4: Greater is He in me than in the world.

- John 8:36: So if the Son sets you free, you will be free indeed. Yeshua and His sacrificial blood are more significant than the prince and the power of the air.

One last example; In verse 34 of Mark 13:32-37, Yeshua is talking with His disciples about the time between His ascension to Heaven, which took place 2,000 years ago (Acts 1:6-11), and the time of His return, which has not happened yet. In other words, Yeshua is talking about the time we are living in.

In verse 34, Yeshua likens Himself to a man who has gone away to a far off country (Heaven). While He is gone, He has given His authority to His servants (you and I). In other words, Yeshua is saying He has given us His authority between His ascension and the time of His return. For a more precise understanding, the Greek word for authority here is *exousia,* which means that we received the following:

- He gave us the power He had.
- He gave us the ability He had.
- He gave us the authority He had.

We have the same power, ability, and authority over the devil, demons, sickness, and disease that our Messiah has.

> The blood is more than an equalizer against the devil; it is the liberator. Yet, the stalwart's belief that believers can be demon-possessed is not found in the New Testament.

There is a story of a stag that roamed about with the utmost security wherever it wanted to go because of the label on its neck, "Touch me not, I belong to Caesar." No one dared touch the horse. Similarly, the faithful servants of God are always safe, for the enemy fears the name of God over our lives through the shed blood of Yeshua. All creation revers the awe of God. How much more does this hold for the redeemed in the blood of Yeshua.

11

SOUL WORK OR DEVIL WORK

THE THESIS OF THIS CHAPTER IS THAT WE HAVE MADE SOUL problems into devil problems. This has put the devil front and center in so many lives. Since this is so entrenched in church culture, you likely have formulated the same perspective. In most cases, this is nothing more than a road of more frustration, and an interrupter of the Glory.

How did the faith community get into this place where the devil and demons are seen as the cause and effect for almost every problem in the believer's life?

The plain truth is there is an overemphasis on the devil, (deliverance and demons). If I was medically misdiagnosed by a well-trained, intelligent medical doctor that led to a fatal heart attack, pastors, leaders, and laypeople could make the same spiritual mistake because it takes spiritual discernment to determine someone's spiritual disease. Too many people are spiritually misdiagnosed because they lack the understanding of the power of the blood of Yeshua. We need to understand what the Word says and what it doesn't say. Learn again what the devil can do, and what he can't do. I will say here and now that the devil is acutely overrated in a believer's life. In a sense, we have given the devil an office in the Church.

So, I ask that you now lift your chin a little higher. The Glory is still here, and it will meet you as you climb higher with a new curiosity. I will formulate the idea in a new way, but it is an old adversary. We will put this old devil back in the proverbial bottle and throw him out to sea. Know also, that all of my comments concern those covered in the blood of Yeshua.

Before I drill down into our chapter title, I know there are large-scale opinions in our church culture over this topic. I have said plainly that believers cannot be demon-possessed, demon oppressed, or victimized by demonic assignments from the devil, whether it be witchcraft or sorcery. Sorcerers and witches may exercise their craft against a child of God, but it amounts to nothing. They have no power because they have no authority.

Yet, situations can arise where one turns back to darkness, as stated in Hebrews 6. Dark things come to those who backslide and lose their first love (Revelation 2:4). If one continues to live in sin and makes it a practice (1 John 3:8-9), a door to the devil's craft opens. Yeshua Himself said in Matthew 7:16-20 (NKJV):

> *You will know them by their fruits.... A good tree cannot bear bad fruit, nor can a bad tree bear good fruit. Every tree that does not bear good fruit is cut down and thrown into the fire. Therefore by their fruits you will know them.*

One can grieve and quench the Holy Spirit (Ephesians 4:30; 1 Thessalonians 5:19; Hebrews 10:29) because the Holy Spirit is a divine person and part of the Triune Godhead (Matthew 28:19; 2 Corinthians 13:14). He is our Helper and Teacher (Romans 8:26-27; John 16:14). At the same time, the Holy Spirit is the Glory too. *"If ye be reproached for the name of Yeshua, happy are ye; for the spirit of glory and of God resteth upon you..."* (1 Peter 4:14 KJV). When we understand that the Holy Spirit is a Person with a divine personality and emotion, stewarding the Glory becomes important, as understanding the soul is important in our life. New learning is once again around the corner.

TWO SISTERS: SODOM AND GOMORRAH

The soul and the devil are like the Biblical Sodom and its sister Gomorrah. These two cities sat on a beautiful plain near the Jordan River. Although they became the epitome of depravity, Sodom and Gomorrah committed many crimes: Her daughters were arrogant, overfed, and unconcerned. Sounds like the soul to me, and the devil has a bad reputation every bit as bad as Gomorrah.

Yet we have not separated these two twins in the church by making soul issues into devil issues, thereby working the devil, and the devil works us. After all, all our problems must be the devil, right?

For instance, ask for help with fear, depression, hopelessness, doubt, etc., it's the devil trying to rob you, a demonic conspiracy against you, the devil is trying to steal your calling, demons have been sent to hinder you. Would it surprise you that the psalmist struggled with many of these same emotions as the apostle Paul and us today? In times past, rarely were those struggles attributed to the devil. Yet, we insist on seeing a distorted view, because tradition has put a scratch on the lens of our eyesight that affects our perception of life's struggles.

The psalmist and Paul didn't have this distorted view of assigning cause and effect to demons and the devil. Paul understood the devil's work in the world. Still, they both followed in 2 Corinthians 10:5, by casting down imaginations and every high thing that seeks to exalt itself against the knowledge of God, and brought into captivity every thought to the obedience of Yeshua. They took their souls captive by immediately meditating on things useful to their spiritual life.

Consider. Paul states in Hebrews 4:12 (KJV):

> *For the word of God is quick, and powerful, and sharper than any two edged sword, piercing even to the dividing asunder of soul and spirit, and of the joints and marrow, and is a discerner of the thoughts and intents of the heart.*

Both Paul and the psalmist channeled their soul upward and away from their carnal hold. Let's review some of the psalmist's problems.

- Psalm 6:3 (KJV): *"My soul is also sore vexed: but thou, O LORD, how long?"* Troubled. Fear. Worry.

- Psalm 13:2 (KJV): *"How long shall I take counsel in my soul, having sorrow in my heart daily? How long shall mine enemy be exalted over me?"* Listening to his mind, or soul, his thoughts.

- Psalm 41:4 (KJV): *"I said, LORD, be merciful unto me: heal my soul; for I have sinned against thee."* Conviction. Remorse. Guilt.

- Psalm 42:5 (KJV): *"Why art thou cast down, O my soul? And why art thou disquieted in me? Hope thou in God: for I shall yet praise him for the help of his countenance."* Quietness and trouble in his soul.

- Psalm 42:4-5: *"Why, my soul, are you downcast? Why so disturbed within me? Put your hope in God, for I will yet praise him, my Savior and my God."* Hopelessness. Depressed. Disturbed.

- Psalm 42:6 (KJV): *"O my God, my soul is cast down within me: therefore will I remember thee from the land of Jordan, and of the Hermonites, from the hill Mizar."* Depressed. Fearful.

- Psalm 42:5-6 (NLT): *"Why am I discouraged? Why is my heart so sad? I will put my hope in God! I will praise him again—my Savior and my God!"*

GOING THE DISTANCE

A classic devil scripture is in 2 Corinthians 10:5: "We demolish arguments and every pretension that sets itself up against the knowledge of God, and we take captive every thought to make it obedient to Christ." Are these thoughts from the devil or our souls?

The meaning of this passage has nothing to do with the devil, but with our souls. Read carefully. "*And every high-minded thing raised against God's knowledge, taking every* thought *captive to obey Christ. Or "bringing down* reasonings, *and every high and lofty* thought *lifted against the* knowledge *of God and bringing into captivity* every thought *to the obedience of the Christ*" (Literal translation).

Another classic example is Ephesians 5, which deals with Christian living and then follows in chapter 6. After having laid before them the high calling and the great doctrines of the Gospel, Paul reveals how we remain overcomers. After all, we live in a world ruled by the prince and the power of the air (Ephesians 2:2; 2 Corinthians 4:4). So, let's be strong in the Lord and His mighty power. Put on the whole armor of God, stand, have our loins girt with truth, put on the breastplate of righteousness, have our feet shod with the preparation of the Gospel of peace, take up the shield of faith, the helmet of salvation, and the sword of the Spirit (Ephesians 6:10-18).

In sum, be strong and increase in strength.[1] Rather than victims of the devil, we are conquerors (Romans 8:37) taking the kingdom of darkness for the Kingdom of light. Persevering, spiritually motoring forward.

DEVIL'S CROSS TRAFFIC

Life in the Kingdom is like the constant cross traffic on the highway. The devil is always going in the opposite direction of the glorious life in Yeshua. We see it daily, and if we stay in our lane, Kingdom living is driving defensively so there is little chance of a spiritual collision. But Yeshua said plainly, "I am sending you out like sheep among wolves. Therefore be as shrewd as snakes and as innocent as doves" (Matthew 10:16). And although this sacred Glory life is a celebration, celebrations can also turn sour. The Kingdom is always under external and internal resistance and metaphysical pressure—light against the darkness, good against evil, etc.

> The best antidote to this internal resistance is persistence, and to the metaphysical pressure is knowing our authority and identity.

First John 4:4 (NLT) says, "the Spirit who lives in you is greater than the spirit who lives in the world." And John 8:36 (ESV) tells us, *"So if the Son sets you free, you will be free indeed."* Yeshua and His sacrificial blood are more significant than the prince and the power of the air. To repeat what was stated already, when Yeshua rose from the dead, His power fell like lightning from the sky (Luke 10:18), and our Lord's authority fell like an anvil crushing Satan's head. He was condemned to crawling on the dust of the earth all the days of his life (Genesis 3:14).

NOTE

1. See Philippians 4:13; 2 Timothy 4:17; 2:1; Romans 4:20; Ephesians 6:10; Hebrews 11: 34; Acts 9:22.

12

DIVINE ARCHITECTURE

WHEN I WAS A YOUNG MAN, I ENJOYED TAKING THINGS apart and putting them back together. When I died and went to Heaven and returned to life, something similar occurred: A personal disassembly. Something else. A small part of me went missing, like the washer of a bolt, not observable from the outside, but nothing would be the same. My spirit, soul, and body are no longer as tightly connected.

Dancing Past the Darkness asks us to take the pieces apart to understand our soul's design, learn what our soul needs, and how our soul affects our lives. Without getting too technical, I want to take you on a stroll through your soul. Living in the Glory requires us to care of our souls, and understand its relationship to the Spirit.

As vividly as possible, I wish to recall what God revealed out of the glory. It is a topic that for over 45 years of faith, I have never heard taught in the Church. This began to guide me from situation to situation as I was mastering a new discipline. Soon, I was feeling a vast openness rather than that ceiling feel. I was out of the cocoon of tradition and convention, and I learned not only who I am, but what I am. The imprint of Heaven remained fresh, and the immense struggles of this world transported themselves off and away from my soul. You will see how important this topic is in walking in the Glory.

When we come to faith, we all come scarred from life's winces and experiences to one degree or another. Perhaps how one looks at another reminds them of their mother or father; a painful memory lingers from childhood to adulthood. The good news is the Good News! These things from the past no longer have impunity once we come to faith. The Spirit begins a healing process as it moves us toward spiritual and emotional health.

This is because the soul is a silhouette of our internal state; it determines who we are and how we live. The soul is like a catch-basin or net that traps all the experiences in life, the good, the bad and the ugly. These play a role in a vast network of feelings, emotions, will, and our intellect. In Greek, it is *psuche,* and together with *ology* we have the world of psychology. In Hebrew, it is *nefesh,* meaning soul. *Nefesh HaChaim,* is living soul in Hebrew.

Shakespeare wrote that the "eye is a window into the soul." The same idea is expressed in Matthew 6:22-23, *"The eye is the lamp of the body. If your eyes are healthy, your whole body will be full of light. But if your eyes are unhealthy, your whole body will be full of darkness. If then the light within you is darkness, how great is that darkness!"*

> We learn that what occurs in the soul has consequences on how we live, and it has nothing to do with demons or the devil.

In fact, our lives are situated within a theatre of feelings and emotions. More is discussed in the next chapter, but that's why the Bible states that *"The heart is deceitful above all things, and desperately sick; who can understand it?"* (Jeremiah 17:9 ESV). Or *"Whoever trusts in his own mind [soul] is a fool, but he who walks in wisdom will be delivered"* (Proverbs 28:26 ESV). One is natural, and the other is supernatural.

DIVINE DESIGN

Each one of us is a three-part unit of spirit, soul, and body. The illustration above shows every individual's three operating parts that's all happening backroom if you will. In Jewish understanding, we are a composite of two equal amounts but opposite or opposing elements: body and soul. Since they are similar, neither can overcome the other.

In Judaism, it is believed that on Sabbath, a Jew receives a *neshama yetera,* an additional soul, so the two cannot confront the body—this added *neshema* (breath) can now subdue the body, and the mind will be open to learning Torah, and spiritual pursuits will be possible. Of course, this is a fanciful explanation that leaves out an important reality—the presence of the Holy Spirit. They still cannot solve the mystery of the conflict between soul and body, which can only be solved with our faith in Messiah, and the indwelling of the Holy Spirit.

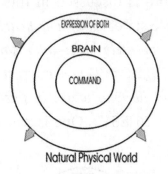

Natural Physical World

Following this pattern of thought, picture the Spirit as the command center—the soul the brain center—the body the physical out-working of the Spirit and soul. The soul can either be driven by the Spirit of God or our carnal nature. As the Spirit connects him to his relationship with God, the soul is enclothed within the body, allowing a man to reveal God through His divine presence.

- The Spirit commands the soul to worship, so we raise our hands to honor Him.

- The spirit stimulates the soul, and the body must obey the soul's commands.

- The Spirit can trigger the body and soul in a new order—faith. Smith Wigglesworth said, "Fear is to look; faith is to jump, stand still, and know He is God."

Paul reveals the same. The Spirit of God through faith, has infused our whole being with a new spirit called our spirit man (Proverbs 20:27; Ephesians 4:23; 2 Corinthians 5:17), and it has given his soul a brand-new desire.

> *"Do you not know that your body is a temple of the Holy Spirit who is in you, whom you have from God, and you are not your own? For you were bought with a price; therefore glorify God in your body"* (1 Corinthians 6:19-20 NKJV).
>
> *"For as the body apart from the spirit is dead, so also faith apart from works is dead"* (James 2:26 ESV).

Excellent, we say! Supernatural? Yes! All of this is miraculously an up-to-the-minute activity consolidated into a unified process, that was miraculously created by God.

> Now, the body and soul must follow in good—the mind needs to be more robust—the body needs to be weaker—the spirit needs to take more dominion over the body and soul (see 1 Corinthians 12:15-26).

Our outer part contains the soul, the soul is the part that has the spirit, and the body is our visible part where our physical senses dwell—you are a spirit living in a biological body. Psalm 139:14 states, "I praise you because I am fearfully and wonderfully made; your works are wonderful, I know that full well." Did you know that you are the highest order of God's creation on earth, and His most excellent concealment of Himself, until you become born again? Then you receive a spirit from God, and that Spirit comes alive unto God's purposes (Romans 8:10).

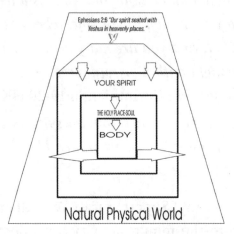

The quintessence of this inside-out life, is illustrated in the following. *"For the kingdom of God is within you"* (Luke 17:20-21 NKJV). *"Above all else, guard your heart, for everything you do flows from it"* (Proverbs 4:23). Your heart is your life.

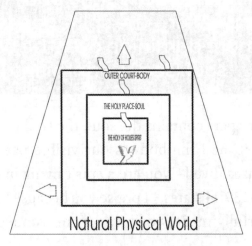

As seen in the diagrams on the former page, we are changed from the inside out as we live our new life in the Kingdom. Experts on holistic health have long determined that all disease comes from the gut; what you take in determines physical health. This is true spiritually; garbage in and garbage out. And although we live and move from the inside out, we are fed from the outside in—changed from the inside.

HOLY OF HOLIES

In the temple, the High Priest had to maintain the golden candlestick, the Menorah, the Table of Incense, the place of prayer and worship, and the table of Show Bread, which represented the Bread of Life—daily, feeding on the Word of God. Our soul is moved from that inner Holy Place by the Spirit of God. It's where we begin to animate our lives for His Glory in the material world. Many scriptural truths depict the inside-out life.

Part of this inside out life is a Holy of Holies space within our soul, just like the ancient Tabernacle. This spiritual holy space fills the vacuum left by the pervasive effects of sin, and begins to heal the tears in the fabric of our souls. The soul then begins to act like a sponge, soaking up the new divine information, the Glory, and the power of the Holy Spirit. As it begins to form new memories, a spiritual mapping is underway, making new-life reference points that transform us into Yeshua's character—the frequency between the spirit and the soul comes alive!

THREE THRONES

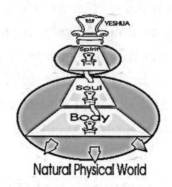

A hidden world begins to break through here, as a world of Glory is waiting to come out of you. As we live from the inside out, we are fed from the outside in. Reading the Word of God—faith cometh by hearing and hearing by the Word of God—discipleship, mentoring, listening, and worship. Constantly the soul and body are in partnership to conform our Spirit toward the Spirit of Yeshua (Ephesians 2:6). But we also have another conundrum too.

Balance in life!

Right diet!

Stewarding our soul!

Four influence centers are constantly flexing for dominance. How do you handle those three thrones? But I should add one more: the Messiah.

1. **Throne of the Messiah**—His Living Word

2. **Throne of the Spirit**—The spirit man

3. **Throne of the Soul**—Free will, cravings, wants, desires, impulses

4. **Throne of the Body**—Physical needs, cravings, and desires.

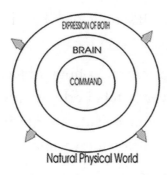

Natural Physical World

We already noted on page 110 that the spirit is the command center, the soul is the brain center—and the body animates the soul's command. Each part or throne contends for influence. Ideally, all are driven by the Messiah and the Word of God. But it's a process, isn't it?

We must learn to pay attention to how things feel physically, spiritually, and emotionally. The body is a formidable foe, craving and flexing its muscles to get what it wants. For example, you have determined to go on a seven-day fast. Two days into the fast, the body begins longing food, seeking to throw you off track; it's trying to usurp the spirit because the body is accustomed to having what it needs and wants.

Will you surrender?

Will you stay or will you go?

While in your fast, you're walking to work when a marvelous aroma of a hot breakfast catches your nose. You see it in your mind's eye as the nose hooks the scent trail, ready to swing you in its direction.

Will you surrender?

Will you stay or will you go?

The soul says, "It's only one bagel." I'll get back on track later.

You decided to join a 24-hour prayer watch. It's 10-12 hours into the prayer watch, perhaps only 4, and your body is exacting sleep—your eyelids are getting heavy, blinking incessantly. I need a little shuteye, and I will resume.

Will you surrender?

Will you stay or will you go?

Take, for example, addictions such as alcoholism, drugs, pornography, and obesity. These cause chemical changes in the brain, and are responsible for destructive behaviors. Now the body becomes the beast that must be fed. But the body has no intelligence—it reacts, responds, animates, and craves. You see, our choices set our lives to live in these bodies in a certain way. Having my life given back, I have a greater responsibility to care for it to give Him glory.

> In conclusion: a holy synergy exists between the spirit, soul, and body for the whole man to come under God's rule and glory.

MORE ON THRONES

Residing in each of us, owed exclusively to the Adamic fall, is our soul that always wants to go rogue. Paul's letter to the Romans: "For what I want to do I do not do, but what I hate I do. ...For I know that good itself does not dwell in me" (Romans 7:15,18). He is speaking about the inherent rogue nature of the soul and the body's promptings. "For I have the desire to do what is good, but I cannot carry it out" (Romans 7:18).

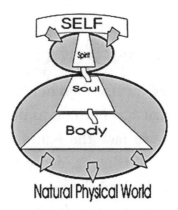

Natural Physical World

Hence, *self* is our most crucial influence center with its program of self-satisfaction. The unhinged soul will drive the body to overeat and find pleasure in drugs, alcohol, and overwork. The soul can enslave the body to the fear of man and the approval of man; tax the body to pursue ego-driven goals formed by the world, or out of poor self-esteem.

What do we learn?

Self wants to rule our lives, but we're to be led by our spirit. Our self needs to be put under subjection, and we must pull the legs out from under its throne. Believers who live predominantly soulishly are guided and ruled more by their souls.

- Their life flow is soul, body, spirit.

- God's order is spirit, soul, body.

Do you notice the difference and its effects on living?

Galatians 5:17 says, *"For the flesh* [soul] *desires what is contrary to the Spirit, and the Spirit what is contrary to the flesh."* Notice, the Galatians text is not a devil issue but a *soul* issue. The psalmist repeatedly addresses his soul: *"Why, O my soul, are you troubled?"*

CONCLUSION

If in the soul our self dwells, then our soul puts acute pressure on our lives that has nothing to do with the devil or his demons. When we face the issues of our soul, anger, bitterness, lack of self-control, depression, fear, etc., we meet our true Goliaths, and the mountains that need to be removed. Again, these are not demonic moves against us, demons, assignments, or curses. Look at your soul, and you discover your work.

13

CARING FOR YOUR VINEYARD

AS SHOWN IN THE ILLUSTRATION AGAIN, WE ARE MADE OF three parts, as discussed in the former chapters. Your soul is the bridge between the body and spirit, therefore you are its caretaker. Essentially, you become the master of mindfulness. Like letting go of things to bring freedom. Or, clinging to anything and everything the wind blows in, only brings anxiety, anger, disappointment, and frustration. Yeshua taught us to purge or avoid the physical and emotional triggers of negativity and obsession that bring feelings that can be controlling. The key is casting down imaginations (2 Corinthians 10:5-7); ridding ourselves of fear and anger (James 1:19-20).

The central purpose of *Heaven's Soul Cleanse* and *A Rabbi's Journey to Heaven,* is dealing with our inner life as we live from the inside out. This touches upon self or soul care through implementing the life of *Dancing Past the Darkness*. This includes a key to daily living in the Glory—face your *soul and* face your actual work.

This inner life is referred to in the Great Commandment: *"Love the Lord your God with all your heart, and with all your soul, and with all your strength, and with all your mind; and your neighbor as yourself"* (Luke 10:27 NASB). Paul writes in Hebrews 4:12 (KJV), *"The word of God is...sharper than any two-edged sword, piercing even to the dividing asunder of soul and spirit."* The Word mediates the conflict, and arrests the flexing behavior of the *soul*. The palmist judges his *soul similarly*.

> To make matters words, we can experience up to 34,000 emotions and sensations.[1] It is estimated that there are around 86 billion neurons in the brain.

Given this vast network of feelings, it doesn't take long to recognize that we can experience an emotional gauntlet in life. Feelings can mislead us. And not all good feelings are good, and not all bad feelings are bad. Drinking alcohol might make someone feel good, but it can be terrible for physical and spiritual health. The weight of guilt over something we have done feels awful, but the discomforting presence of conviction and remorse is good. It feels terrible when we endure seasons of trial, but God's hand is crafting something good from it.

Watchman Nee gave a summary of the soul, which he believed was composed of the mind, enabling us to think, reason, consider, remember, and wonder; all the emotions which will allow us to have feelings like happiness, sorrow, anger, relief, and compassion; and finally, our will which enables us to choose and make decisions. These three—our mind, emotion, and will, make up our personality.

So, we see that we are far more than a marionette doll whose strings are pulled by God or the devil. Our challenge is learning to be spirit-driven, not soul-driven, and differentiating between spirits and emotions. Ponder the difficulties of psalmist:

> Psalm 13:2 (NKJV): *"How long shall I take counsel in my soul, having sorrow in my heart daily? How long shall mine enemy be exalted over me?"*

He's saying, how long shall I listen to my mind (soul). He has heavy sorrow and finds difficulty shaking free of it in his heart. He is troubled at the victory of the unrighteous—fear, frustration, imagination, carnal thoughts.

> Psalm 41:4 (KJV): *"I said, 'LORD, be merciful unto me: heal my soul; for I have sinned against thee."*

He feels remorse and conviction. He pleads with God to heal the separation between his soul and God. It has continued for some time, feeling conviction, remorse, and guilt.

> Psalm 42:4: *"Why, my soul, are you downcast? Why so disturbed within me? Put your hope in*

God, for I will yet praise him, my Savior and my God."

WHAT THE PSALMIST SAW

The psalmist saw a man's soul poverty-stricken, dark, and grey, but also with a capacity to revere God deeply. The psalmist spoke directly to his soul. Then, amid the 66 books of the Bible, I discovered the "Handbook to the Soul." 60 psalms, and 225 verses later, I learned how to channel my soul upward. This part of the Bible would serve as my instruction for not 30 days but over two years. I noticed the following:

- The soul can be estranged from the womb (58:3).

- The soul waits and thirsts for God (62:1-2; 63:1-2).

- The soul needs to cling to God (63:8).

- The soul needs to hear what God has done (66:16).

- God draws near to the soul and gladdens the soul (69:18).

- He commands his soul to bless the Lord (103:1-5).

- The soul was created to worship the Lord in the splendor of His majesty (Psalm 96).

Proverbs 20:27 (KJV) says, *"The spirit* [soul] *of man is the candle of the LORD."* Harness the soul; Yeshua is glorified.

In other words, whenever you choose to make known the will of God, the soul there goeth, and this candle of the Lord burns brighter. *"The spirit* [soul] *of man is the candle of the Lord,"* according to Proverbs 20:27.

One day during the first trimester of my return, the Lord brought me down into the darkness of a man's soul. I felt as if I was walking in the hall of images in the Temple in the book of Ezekiel. Those horrible images of sin, and idol worship were inscribed in a room in the Holy Temple. On the walls of this man's soul, hung the emotional traumas of his life. His soul was dark and felt like a jail cell, frankly. I felt the weightiness of the prevailing darkness.

Similarly, as I noted in previous chapters, we come to faith with specific "soul conditions" after life's good and bad experiences (1 Corinthians 9:19). But, once we focus on the soul as the culprit, we face the true villain, and there is an opportunity to flood the dark areas of our soul with light.

Paul illustrates this in Hebrews 4:12 (KJV):

> *For the word of God is quick, and powerful, and sharper than any two edged sword, piercing even to the dividing asunder of soul and spirit, and of the joints and marrow, and is a discerner of the thoughts and intents of the heart.*

For over three years now, I have learned to channel my soul upward to Heaven, daily taking my soul into a depth it has never experienced before. I have come to know why an angel stood over my spirit when it left my body. Soul work! My life would be poured out for soul work!

NOTE

1. D. Pollack, Plutchik's *Wheel of Emotions Cheat Sheet*, 2016.

14

PAUL'S THORN

WHY IS THE SUBJECT OF PAUL'S THORN IN A BOOK ABOUT the glory, as well as a chapter on Matthew 11:12, the kingdom suffereth violence? Imagine dancing past the darkness when you believe that sickness can be sent to keep you humble or a messenger of Satan to harass you. To return to kingdom normalcy, we need to close every access door of wrong teaching into our soul. Here you will learn to silence these teachings, shunning them from your life.

Recall that if one believes that the days of miracles have ended, the glory will not move when the King of Glory wants to activate in you. During the time of Jesus, those familiar with him, particularly those from His hometown, and the attitudes of the Pharisees radiated unbelief throughout the miracles that He performed. Wrong knowledge existed. Jesus could not do miracles in His hometown due to the same.

Hence, two areas of our focus are Matthew 11:12 (NKJV), *"The kingdom of heaven suffers violence, and violent take it by force."* But what was Paul's thorn?

Paul was bigger than life, he became a towering figure who cast a shadow of greatness over the extraordinary advancement of the Gospel. I cannot help but feel the echoes of him as I walk through the Scriptures. I often sense an adrenaline spike grabbing me to come closer. But then, I confront the infamous thorn! The sharp underside of this man causes us to inquire about this mystery.

One of the most frequent questions I receive when teaching spiritual warfare is over this messenger of Satan sent to torment Paul in 2 Corinthians 12:7. After all, if we have complete authority over the devil, which we do, how do we explain Paul's thorn? This topic has been debated, and is the subject of conjecture and imaginary theories. I have heard that the thorn was temptation, a chronic eye problem, malaria, migraines, epilepsy, and a speech disability. Some have attributed the case to Alexander the coppersmith, who was the source of great harm to Paul (2 Timothy 4:14). Then some say we are completely at a loss because the Bible doesn't reveal the mystery of the thorn.

As noted above, some claim Paul suffered from eye problems based upon Galatians 4:15, "Where, then, is your blessing of me now? I can testify that, if you could have done so, you would have torn out your eyes and given them to me." But Paul had just returned from being stoned and left for dead. Imagine what he looked like. When they stoned people, they hurled large rocks at their faces. Their heads and every part of their bodies were slammed to kill them. Paul had to look horribly bloody and wounded (Acts 14:19-28). The Galatians used a figure of speech as we would today, "if

I can only give you my right arm," but eye. His eyes had been swollen, his face engorged, and his lips likely distended. Perhaps Paul was beyond recognition. Many also believe Paul uses a metaphor that he did not elaborate on, so we must rest in that.

Ultimately, we are left with no clear understanding but for our own curiosity to dissolve, and the road ends. But then, we go one step further.

> The first thing that I notice in this passage is that nowhere is sickness, disease, or poor eyesight mentioned as his thorn.

A sickness of some kind would be baffling, because God does not send disease or a messenger of Satan. If it were a sickness, the very foundation for healing would collapse.[1] Take an individual with multiple conditions. Should we first determine which illness was sent by the devil and allowed by God to humble us?

- Which one should we pray for to be healed?
- If there is only one disease, God might be using it to keep us humble.

We also have a problem with Paul's legacy. Here is a man that was given authority over every sickness and disease (Mark 10:1; Luke 9:1). So, the thorn cannot be a sickness, and nowhere in the Bible is a "thorn" associated with an illness.

PROPER EXEGESIS

In any Biblical study, when we confront an unclear word or phrase like Paul's thorn, the answer is found either in the context or elsewhere. The first clue is in 2 Corinthians 12:10 (Amplified): *"So, I am well pleased with weaknesses, insults, distresses, persecutions, and difficulties, for the sake of Christ. When I am weak [in human strength], then I am strong...."* But this alone is insufficient because we must circle back to the Old Testament to see how "thorn in the flesh" is used."

Let's keep looking.

> *But if you do not drive out the inhabitants of the land from before you, then those whom you let remain shall be as barbs in your eyes and thorns in your sides, and they shall trouble you in the land where you dwell. And I will do to you as I thought to do to them* (Numbers 33:55-56 ESV).

In this passage, God gives Moses instructions for the conquest of Canaan. In verse 55, God tells Moses that if he failed to drive out the land's inhabitants, the people of Canaan would become *"thorns in your sides."* The thorn was from a group of people and an evil nation.

From another passage:

> *For if you turn back and cling to the remnant of these nations remaining among you and make marriages with them, so that you associate with*

*them, know for certain that the LORD your God
will no longer drive out these nations before you,
but they shall be a snare and a trap for you, a whip
on your sides and thorns in your eyes until you
perish from off this good ground that the LORD
your God has given you* (Joshua 23:12-13 ESV).

Joshua here is giving his farewell address, warning the people that if they do not remain separated from the people of the nations they conquered, these people will become *"thorns in their eyes."* Once again, the thorn comes from a group of people, an ungodly nation, but not disease or sickness. Another use of the word "thorns" comes from Proverbs 15:19 (KJV), *"The way of the slothful man is as an hedge of thorns: but the way of the righteous is made plain."*

In Proverbs 22:5 (KJV), *"Thorns and snares are in the way of the froward: he that doth keep his soul shall be far from them."*[2]

WHAT WAS THE THORN?

It was not a messenger of Satan, an attack from demons, a curse from God, or an eye problem or temptation. Perhaps you can already surmise what the source of Paul's thorn was. For greater context let's turn to Acts 9:10-12 (NKJV):

Now, there was a certain disciple at Damascus named Ananias; and to him the Lord said in a vision, "Ananias." And he said, "Here I am, Lord." So the Lord said to him, "Arise and go to the street called Straight, and inquire at the house of Judas for one called Saul of Tarsus, for

*behold, he is praying. And in a vision, he has seen
a man named Ananias coming in and putting his
hand on him, so that he might receive his sight."*

Then, Ananias answered, *"Lord, I
have heard from many about this
man, how much harm he has done
to your saints in Jerusalem. And
here he has authority from the
chief priests to bind all who call
on your name"* (Acts 9:13-14 NKJV).

*But the Lord said to him, "Go, for he is a chosen
vessel of Mine to bear My name before Gentiles, kings, and the children of Israel. For I will
show him how many things he must suffer for My
name's sake." And Ananias went his way and
entered the house; and laying his hands on him,
he said, "Brother Saul, the Lord Yeshua, who
appeared to you on the road as you came, has sent
me that you may receive your sight and be filled
with the Holy Spirit." Immediately there fell from
his eyes something like scales, and he received his
sight at once; and he arose and was baptized. So
when he had received food, he was strengthened.
Then Saul spent some days with the disciples at
Damascus (Acts 9:15-19 NKJV).*

WHAT THINGS DID PAUL SUFFER?

Well, besides utter disrespect and violence at the hands of his own people, it left Paul in constant hurt like a corkscrew twisting through him. His people were constantly crashing into him, pulling him toward their evil intent to harm him, never really yanking free from them. Yet all along, he pressed on because he loved them. Furthermore, anyone in Jewish ministry can somewhat relate to it. Paul writes:

> *I sometimes think God has put us apostles on display, like prisoners of war at the end of a victor's parade, condemned to die. We have become a spectacle to the entire world—to people and angels alike. Our dedication to the Messiah makes us look like fools, but you claim to be so wise in Messiah! We are weak, but you are so powerful! You are honored, but we are ridiculed. Even now, we go hungry and thirsty, and we don't have enough clothes to keep warm. We are often beaten and have no home. We work wearily with our own hands to earn our living. We bless those who curse us. We are patient with those who abuse us. We appeal gently when evil things are said about us. Yet we are treated like the world's garbage, like everybody's trash—up to the present moment* (1 Corinthians 4:9-13 NLT).

The Phrase: "Must Suffer"

I investigated the phrase *"must suffer"* and discovered more information. It seems there are only two individuals who are spoken of using the words *"must suffer."* One is Yeshua, the other is Paul. Paul's unusual suffering is exposed to our gaze here on this matter of the thorn. Review the following:

> Matthew 16:21 (ESV): *From that time Jesus began to show his disciples that he must go to Jerusalem and suffer many things from the elders and chief priests and scribes, and be killed, and on the third day be raised.*
>
> Mark 8:31 (ESV): *And he began to teach them that the Son of Man must suffer many things and be rejected by the elders and the chief priests and the scribes and be killed, and after three days rise again.*
>
> Luke 17:25 (ESV): *But first he must suffer many things and be rejected by this generation.*
>
> Acts 9:16 (ESV): *For I will show him how much he must suffer for the sake of my name.*
>
> Acts 26:23 (ESV): *that the Christ must suffer and that, by being the first to rise from the dead, he would proclaim light both to our people and to the Gentiles.*

I wish to offer one more passage on Paul's suffering:

Are they Hebrews? So am I. Are they Israelites? So am I. Are they descendants of Abraham? So am I. Are they servants of Yeshua? I know I sound like a madman, but I have served him far more! I have worked harder, been put in prison more often, been whipped times without number, and faced death again and again. Five different times the Jewish leaders gave me thirty-nine lashes. Three times I was beaten with rods. Once I was stoned. Three times I was shipwrecked. Once I spent a whole night and a day adrift at sea. I have traveled on many long journeys. I have faced danger from rivers and robbers. I have faced danger from my own people, the Jews, as well as from the Gentiles. I have faced danger in the cities, in the deserts, and on the seas. And I have faced danger from men who claim to be believers but are not. I have worked hard and long, enduring many sleepless nights. I have been hungry and thirsty and have often gone without food. I have shivered in the cold without enough clothing to keep me warm (2 Corinthians 11:22-27 NLT).

Notice, again and again, that disease and sickness are never mentioned. Paul's thorn came from the persecution he faced from his people for preaching the gospel.

No matter how long I mulled it over, no reasonable explanation presented itself except the following. When Paul said that a "messenger of Satan" was sent to him, it was not a doctrinal statement. It described the evil carnal attacks that can be characterized as a messenger of Satan that was always present. Indeed, individuals and people bent on our destruction can be called a messenger of Satan.

CONCLUSION

Paul was familiar with the term from the Jewish Old Testament, of which he was a scholar. He knew that a thorn represented a people or a person, and was acutely aware of the history of Moses, and Joshua. Thorn was a metaphor commonly used in Jewish writings to point to a person or people, as such as the evil condition of the Pharisees and their ongoing, constant oppression. They represented an emotional juggernaut constantly.

Paul had to be weary from their persecution and resistance, just like Moses wearied at times with the Israelites. Out of frustration with his people, Moses struck the rock at Meribah instead of speaking to it as God commanded him. His people were a thorn in his side many times, not by persecution but by annoyance, complaining, and quarreling.[3]

I discovered a deeper realization with Paul's suffering that burned like an ember constantly in him. Paul felt at times like the light was draining from the sky, and crashing of waves of frustration were drowning him. But continually Paul showed God and the world what he could do when

God's grace was sufficient. God said to Paul, my grace would be sufficient—he would have to deal with it and press on.

NOTES

1. Mark 5:34; James 5:14-16; 1 Peter 2:24; Psalm 103:1-5; Psalm 147:2-4; Matthew 4:23; 8:16-17; 9:35; 10:7-8; Luke 6:17-19; 12:17-19; 13:11-13; 14:1-6

2. Judges 2:3 (NKJV): *"Therefore I also said, 'I will not drive them out from before you; but they shall be as thorns in your side, and their gods shall be a snare to you."*
    Ezekiel 28:24 (KJV): *"And there shall be no more a pricking brier unto the house of Israel, nor any grieving thorn of all that are round about them, that despised them; and they shall know that I am the Lord GOD."*

3. Exodus 5:21; 14:11-12; 15:24; 16:2,7-9,12; 17:3; Numbers 11:1-6; 14:2; 16:11; 17:5; 20:1-13; 21:4-9; Deuteronomy 1:27; Psalm 106:25

15

KINGDOM SUFFERETH VIOLENCE

...the kingdom of heaven suffereth violence,
and the violent take it by force
(Matthew 11:12 KJV).

WHO IS "THE VIOLENT"?

Once again, the topic of our discussion in this chapter and the former, it does not fit the flow topic of the glory that we have been enjoying. But the King of Glory said, the Kingdom of Heaven and all its glory suffereth violence. It portrayed a coming Kingdom subject to immense persecution where one world is colliding against the other—one heavenly and glorious, the other mortal and aberrant—one ruled by God, the other by the prince and power of the air. Satan would do everything to thwart the Glory, and that is why we must discuss it.

In this world, our struggles can be summed up in Ephesians 6:12-13, that our battle is not against flesh and blood, but between spiritual powers in heavenly places; therefore put on the full armor of God. (See also in Matthew 11:12). From the onset of the Kingdom of which John was the chosen herald, violence began.

- King Herod arrested John the Baptist and had him beheaded.

- Violent opposition rises against Yeshua Himself, the King of Glory.

- Most of the apostles were martyred for the same reason.

- Paul was confined to a jail cell (Acts 16:16-40).

- Paul was constantly running from those seeking to stone him. He was imprisoned toward the end of his life and beheaded (Acts 20:22-24).

- In Matthew chapter 12, Israel's religious leaders' first conspiracy to take Yeshua's life (see verse 14) was the high point of Israel's resistance, and violence against Yeshua's earthly ministry. Yeshua condemns that generation because they had committed the "unpardonable sin."

Ever since John the Baptist, the world started to grow with deep hatred toward the servants of God. The Glory of God is the devil's thorn, and Paul's difficulties with this principle were epic. All these attacks, though, were remarkable for different reasons. The Gospel found extraordinary improvisation as the Glory and power compelled them forward for the Gospel. But it should be noted that none of this was a demonic intrusion from within. Rather, from the outside world that has been obtrusively evil bent against the work of Glory since John the Baptist.

TRADITIONAL INTERPRETATION

Traditional teaching tells us something else. The Matthew 11:12 interpretation is that believers take the Kingdom by force. I don't recall a passage of Scripture to be the subject of more diverse interpretations, from commentaries to different Bible versions as this one. One says that the force comes from believers, while the other from the devil. Which one is correct? What does it mean then, "and the violent take it by force?"

Most versions say: *"And from the days of John the Baptist until the present time, the kingdom of heaven has endured violent assault, and violent men seize it by force [as a precious prize]...* (Matthew 11:12 Amplified Bible, Classic Edition).

In this view, the heavenly Kingdom requires intense physical force and exertion. And those doing the taking are assumed to be believers, entering the Kingdom of Heaven. But that is not the case if we compare scripture with scripture. Versions such as the Amplified make up only a handful that are correct.

The Kingdom does not come by forceful seizure or robbery, as the word means. Wouldn't it be strange for God's Word to tell believers to be violent and act by force to take the Kingdom of God? Are we to steal the Kingdom, if you will? If that were true, the Bible should say, "And from the days of John the Baptist until now the kingdom of heaven suffered violence and the violent ENTER it by force." Do we enter the Kingdom through violence and force?

I wonder how many over the course of two thousand years, and into the present have entered the kingdom by forceful seizure as robbers stealing it. The question emerges: If that is the case, who are we stealing it from? No! We enter the Kingdom through humility, brokenness, repentance, confession, and love. *"God blesses those who work for peace, for they will be called the children of God"* (Matthew 5:9 NLT). *"Blessed are the gentle, for they shall inherit the earth"* (Matthew 5:5 NASB). This has been the way since the days of John the Baptist. The people in Matthew 11 are not entering the Kingdom of Heaven by taking it or stealing it.

We enter the Kingdom as in Luke 16:16 (KJV), *"The law and the prophets were until John. Since that time the kingdom of God has been preached, and everyone is pressing into it."* Pressing in is entirely different from stealing or forceful violence, as in Matthew 11:12.

CONCLUSION

Parable of the Wicked Husbandman

There was a campaign of intimidation, oppression, and persecution during Messiah's earthly ministry. John is imprisoned only to lose his life. Yeshua will be put to death. Matthew 11:12 talks about lost people taking the Kingdom of Heaven by force, while Luke 16:16 talks about believers pressing in to enter the Kingdom of Heaven. Philippians 3:14 says, *"I press on toward the goal to win the prize for which God has called me heavenward in Christ Yeshua."* But they thought His death would be the end of Him. Of course, we all know the Lord Yeshua did not stay dead! He was resurrected and is coming again to bring Israel's literal, physical, visible, earthly, Davidic Kingdom! Several months after Matthew 21:33-42 (KJ21), there is an answer in the form of a parable:

> *"There was a certain householder, who planted a vineyard, and hedged it round about, and dug a winepress in it, and built a tower, and let it out to husbandmen, and went into a far country: And when the time of the fruit drew near, he sent his servants to the husbandmen, that they might receive the fruits of it. And the husbandmen took his servants, and beat one and killed another and stoned another. Again, he sent other servants, more than the first; and they did unto them likewise. But last, he sent unto them his son, saying, 'They will reverence my son.' But when the husbandmen saw the son, they said among themselves, 'This is the heir. Come, let us kill him, and let us seize on his inheritance.' And they caught him and cast him out of the vineyard, and slew him. When therefore the lord of the vineyard cometh, what will he do unto those husbandmen?"* They said unto Him, *"He will miserably destroy those wicked men, and will let out his vineyard unto other husbandmen who shall render him the fruits in their seasons."* Yeshua said unto them, *"Did ye never read*

in the Scriptures: 'The stone which the build-
ers rejected, the same is become the head of the
corner. This is the Lord's doing, and it is marvel-
ous in our eyes'?

In explaining that parable, Yeshua said that He would come back and destroy those who would take His life; His Second Coming when He returns to set up His Kingdom on the earth. Having reached full circle, we see this as *"the king-dom of heaven"* that John the Baptist preached.

16

FINDING KINGDOM NORMALCY

WE HAVE REFERRED TO KINGDOM NORMALCY through-out this work, it is now time to define it. You'll see what your days can look like, and what Yeshua intended for us.

Knowing you are liberated and joined in the Kingdom of God, what astonishment God's people can cause when we set our course toward Kingdom Normalcy again—a life of greater Glory. We are the soldier bride living in and through the power and Glory of the King of Glory. This Kingdom has been created with a supernatural defense and sustainability for 2,000 years. I found a new excitement as I set my course for Kingdom Normalcy again, as you will see in this chapter.

But let me first tell you what it's not!

It is like a car performing on only half its cylinders. Instead of enjoying the wind racing by on a summer night or enjoying that drive up to those beautiful mountain ranges, you're limited to the slow, flat, and dull lane because you don't have adequate power. This is true of our spiritual life. Too many are spiritually coasting along on half power, never enjoying the full ride with the Holy Spirit.

Kingdom Normalcy believes again in the impossible, having confidence in the Great Physician when we pray for the sick; sharing the Gospel; living daily and letting faith take you where you have not gone before. God has little trouble righting the ship, so we live again in the daily power of the Kingdom.

I recall the early morning when I determined to study Yeshua's universe as my model of Kingdom Normalcy. I wanted to follow in His footsteps. *How can I go wrong?* I thought. Soon, it led to page-turning mornings soaking up every one of His footsteps. I marveled at how He could identify a hidden opportunity in the ordinary course of a day. Yeshua could scrutinize and read people's thoughts and intents of the heart. But He also saw things immediately. He was full of the Glory, and power of the Holy Spirit. Smith Wigglesworth calls this, "divine inflow of the life of God." Seeing this, my perspective changed immediately.

- I saw the Lord interrupt a funeral to bring the deceased back to life (Luke 7:11-17). Imagine stepping into a funeral home for the Kingdom.

- He healed the mother of Peter's wife (Matthew 8:14-15; Mark 1:29-31; Luke 4:38-39); the deafness of Decapolis (Mark 7:31-37);

- The blind from birth were given sight (John 1:9-12; Matthew 15:30-31).

- He healed the paralytic at Bethesda, the blind man of Bethsaida, the blind beggar man Bartimaeus in Jericho, the centurion's servant, and an infirmed woman (Luke 13:10-17), a prostitute at the well getting water (John 4), and Lazarus already in the tomb (John 11:5-6).

All throughout the ordinary course of a day! He said greater works than He shall we do. Friend, Yeshua wasn't just checking the box on Sunday or Saturday. Every day was packed with heavenly opportunities. I needed to slow down in my day, walk slower, scan my audience, be aware of the situation I am in so that the Holy Spirit can move through me in a moment's time. Then following several weeks of study, and going out and modeling His actions, I saw a woman coming out of the restaurant one day who appeared different. Although the woman's brow perhaps arched in surprise, staring blankly at my advances, I realized that the Holy Spirit was on the scene, and she was about to have God's love rain down on her. I shared the Love of God with her, and then she allowed me to pray for her. This pattern repeats itself now daily. Everyday life was becoming familiar, and in some small ways my days were becoming epic. After all, He said, "greater works than He shall we do" (see John 14:12).

BACK-OFFICE FAITH

The problem as I see it, many people's faith could be characterized as back-office, never getting out to share their faith. Their faith is a secret. I can only imagine if Yeshua sacrificed His life privately with no one around to communicate the plan of redemption. Today's church is losing what it once had, regrettably, living in the shadows of the church in

Ephesus in the book of Revelation. They were commended for many things, but stopped doing "First Love" works. They lost a heart for people. Secret faith is a tragedy. It binds many today!

> When normalcy returns, happenings occur in the most unsuspecting places at the most "inconvenient" times—Praise God!

The problem is that people are just too busy and too deep into the wrong universe. That may surprise many, and others will be hooked with conviction. I can see eyebrows twitching, some reaching to scratch like when we're uncomfortable in certain situations.

Right?

But to be more specific.

It's not hard to know that there's this other world we don't get to know enough about anymore because we're too busy. We've lost our bearings, and are no longer engaged in the world. We cannot follow Heaven's GPS (God's Positioning System) because we're too consumed with our own journey. But this other universe, Yeshua's world, wants us activated again. We need warmth in our hearts for the lost again because people need hope. We don't need revival for this, just remember who you are! We need to get out of the back office and onto the floor where the people are, and lost souls fill every corner of our day.

GLORY RAIN BEGINS

The Glory Hits the Parking Lot

Two weeks ago, God told the soldier bride, me, to pull into that parking lot to check things out. So, I did. I had my schedule and my to-do list like everyone else. Still, God said pull into the parking lot! Not for shopping, heavens no! He knows that. He was setting someone up for salvation. Immediately, while parking my car, a woman with an enormous black Newfoundland captured my attention. The dog was a beautiful jet-black color. As I greeted the woman, I didn't miss the edge of interest in her voice by my willingness to say hello. She looked harried as if she'd been running all day, which is not uncommon today. I usually begin, "Excuse me, I wish to simply tell you that God loves you!"

> A simple declarative truth, that would open the door of her heart. Three words: God loves you!

Although I started to tell her how beautiful her dog was, it was the Jewish woman that day who happened to have a black Newfoundland who got saved in Trader Joe's parking lot—the dog was only my divine attention-getter. God does that often, so be alert for God's attention getters in your day.

Now, this is where it gets more exciting and surreal.

Shaking hands together, she presses her palms against mine, and a warm embrace follows, gesturing that something more is to come. From our conversation about Yeshua, she explains that she has never read a Bible in her entire life.

Imagine a woman living three-quarters of her life never opening a Bible in America! "Being Jewish, it wasn't the thing to do," she said. I understood. Then I excused myself and proceeded to my car, where I had my personal Bible with all the Messianic prophecies highlighted. When I returned, I offered her my personal Bible to keep. She clutched it tightly to her chest, sending shivers down my spine as though she had found a long-lost treasure. It was beautiful, and surreal! I thought she would sit down then and there read it from cover to cover. She said she would cherish our time together, especially her Bible, for the rest of her life. Today she is in the Kingdom.

Lesson One: We're too consumed with the wrong universe; most wouldn't have stopped. We miss the divine attention getters. I believe they are around you every day, but you pass by them. It's raining, but you don't see it. You're on the mountain, passing the bush, but you don't see the fire.

The Glory Hits the Food Store

I was simply standing in the food store when I sensed the unction of God to walk to the other side to strike a conversation with an individual who caught my attention. I caught a snippet of a discussion about our times between two people. Today, it may not be the woman at the well, two thousand years ago, but the woman on line will get the same thing.

She studied me, and I looked at her, perhaps awkwardly so. It was more like her gaze skimming over my appearance, wondering what I was doing. I step forward to contemplate my new position. I hovered at the edge of that holy action. You know, that tightly timeless choreographed scene. I retract a bit and wonder, *Should I? Is she open?* I'm still staring at her when she stops and looks at me. I begin to say something. And, off we go! God is at work!

> Here is the key: the Holy Spirit organizes you; you don't organize Him. If the Church returned to that simple formula, she would be on her way to being reconstituted up. This is undoubtedly a word—thank You, Lord!

Lesson Two: Be sensitive to Holy queues. Obey the unction of the Spirit and have no fear; be friendly, warm, and caring.

One morning I watched a man standing in the aisle as the Holy Spirit prompted some queues that I later realized I missed. Only to leave and go back into the store to engage him. Now people were congregating in every inch of space. But no matter, Yeshua wouldn't care. Suddenly he begins to understand that perhaps I'm no ordinary guy. I'm not. It's a typical day in an unordinary universe of Yeshua. The man needed prayer for a difficult season in his life. I ask the Lord, "What should I say, Lord?" And off we go, the Kingdom enlarges again. If you are sensitive to the queues, God will use many things to get your attention.

Lesson Three: If you sense you missed a divine opportunity, go back, eternity hangs in the balance.

The Glory Hits The Bronx

Oy vey! Yes, I am lost in the Bronx! The Bronx and its urban vibe would bring unease to many, but I was pierced with a tenderness that morning. I was inching forward bumper to bumper, time was fleeting like a vapor, one red light after another. Most would be irritated. But the Lord turned my head on something else within this sea of humanity. "Remember, you are in MY universe now!" said the Lord.

Within the delay, I marveled at the thousands of potential new creations—a valley of dry bones that could come to life as I prophesied them into faith. With the supernatural impulse of my spirit, I chose what is better over what some may see as an urban jungle. Can you remove distractions and focus on what matters most? Spot it! Act on it!

Across the Word of God, we find multiple teachings concerning detaching from this world. And if we are successful, we will discover life as an *objective observer,* and therein lies the secret. Suddenly, that big black Newfoundland becomes your glaring opportunity. That individual you spotted with eternity in their eyes while shopping prompts you to pray for them. The young man at a truck stop, whose life was interrupted by a strange man that led him to the Lord right behind the cash register while people were waiting on line to pay. Now that is desperation! He shared how he has been bullied his whole life, and I identified the pain in his eyes when I went up to the cash register. This is the core effect of both a Presence-driven life and being detached. What else would you want the glory and a presence-driven life.

WHY CHRISTIANS DON'T WITNESS

You see, no heavenly experience is genuine if it does not liberate one's outward life. Our heart is to live outwardly, demonstrating such fruits as goodness, kindness, and compassion. The central point of this chapter is what the Kingdom produces. Fruit. Evidence. Power. Souls.

Indeed, God desires to give and forgive. And He did, and He does! After all, the whole plan of redemption was set in motion by his sacrifice. We share the word of life to see the lost come to faith, and walk in a Glory presence filled life each day. The less involved in the world's pursuits, the more it sheers away exhaustion, leaving more time and energy to share the most incredible love story ever. We are filled with so many precious blessings from the Lord to be shared. And my experience in Heaven is one of the precious belongings that I will forever share.

Sadly, Christians fail to experience the lost coming to faith because they are too busy, often too fearful, and lack training and experience. But if one never steps out, the experience can never come. Make room in your day; be willing to be used in the lives of a stranger hurting, and those who are those spiritually dying. I'm passionate about this because I have a holy obsession to see souls come into the Kingdom. Far too many fears about sharing the Gospel exist; it has crippled the church and silenced believers. It's time to pick up your sword and wield the word of faith; to bind the spirit of fear. *Stop* the busyness and allow more of God's reign to take hold, so you can experience the joy of seeing someone come into the Kingdom!

CELEBRATION OF FAITH

Faith is a celebration that comes with service. We do not focus upon the things we do or the specific acts of kindness, but on a life of service; we desire to mimic our Lord. Jeremy Taylor said, "Love to be concealed, and little esteemed: be content to want [lack] praise, never be troubled when slighted or undervalued.... Hiddenness is a rebuke to the flesh and can deal a fatal blow to pride."[1]

> What is simplicity? A joyful unconcern for possessions, which has nothing to do with possessions or the lack thereof, but an inward celebration of the spirit of trust.

We learn to cease from showy extravagance, not that you can't afford it, but because of principle. You've abandoned those things that the world's people live for, and you are now content with your station in life. Days are spent not laying up treasures upon the earth, where moth and rust destroy, or where thieves can steal (Matthew 6:19-20). But perhaps, like Dorcas, we're finding ways to make *"coats and garments for widows"* (Acts 9:39).

If I could stress any point it's that the Glory is not merely for the experience. Heavens no! It is for God to save and transform people's lives. Picture what we can do for the Lord and our potential exploits for Him.

NOTE

1. Jeremy Taylor: *The Grace of Humility.*

17

OCCUPY UNTIL
I RETURN

...Occupy till I come! (Luke 19:13 KJV)

GIVEN THE GLORY I EXPERIENCED, YOU WOULD THINK I'M anxious to return to Heaven. You're wrong! God said live. God is the God of life. *La Chaim*—to Life. He gave His only Son for my life. Live your life for Him while you have the day-light and occupy until He comes. *Go back and occupy until I return, said the Lord!*

When it was time to live again, a wind rushed into my mouth, causing me to draw the deepest life-giving breath I have ever taken. It felt like a person submerged underwa-ter who broke through the surface to gasp for air with all his might. But that's not the end of the story, heavens no! The following is what God showed me from Heaven and a mes-sage for our times.

First, God wants you to see the condition of the world. If we could look down across the earth's landscape, we would see humanity fragmented beyond repair. We would see many struggling with competing attachments and devotions. There is a herd of humanity headed off a cliff down into a dark place, and God wants to stop us to spot our opportunities for Him.

Second, God doesn't want you home before your time, with your assignment is incomplete. There is a difference between a complete separation, and a partial. You never want to get to Heaven with your work undone. Be a living advertisement for Him. Know that I am returning soon, and the night is still long, but the day will soon be upon you. Live and carry my message. Live demonstrating my Glory He says; it's part of my message to you from the Lord. I want you to know that I returned to reach out into the depths of your heart with these words. *Go and live the life that God has given you.*

Note: I don't know why this message was given to me. Perhaps someone reading this is struggling with a dark spirit of death and contemplating taking their life. A young person reading this may find themselves in despair, with depression tormenting them. The message to live floods the darkness of your soul with the blinding light of hope. God says to you, "I" love you, and "I" created you for a glorious purpose. Only in "Me" will you find rest for your soul. Turn to "Me," says the Lord, and let "Me" show you the fulfillment and love that your soul desperately deserves.

Third, God does not want you waiting with bated breath for the rapture. No! God is not like a man looking intently through the window for his bride to enter. He knows when you are coming home. He wants His bride to live her life abundantly—He wants you to be the bride of Christ on the earth because His only Son was given for you.

Friend, if you could understand that Heaven was created for you, much of the internal churning and twisting, I believe, would cease. You would be animated again for the Kingdom. It's waiting for you to complete your assignment.

Fourth, I saw a sea of people as trees flushed with fruit falling in baskets, and then distributed. According to Romans 12:6 (KJV), we have been entrusted with abundant gifts for the Lord: *"Having then gifts differing according to the grace given to us."* Our task is to invest our time, talents, and treasures, and use the Lord's opportunities that are given to us. The command to *occupy until He returns* comes with no earthly expiration date as in the secular world. In 2 John 8 (KJV), John admonishes us, *"Look to yourselves, that we lose not those things which we have wrought, but that we receive a full reward."*

Too many Christians start well in the journey, but become disenchanted, discouraged, then detoured for one reason or another. John reminds us that the only way to receive a full reward when we meet the Lord is to continue to the end. The words of an old hymn by Fanny Crosby come to mind:

> When Jesus comes to reward His servants,
> Whether it be noon or night,
> Faithful to Him will He find us watching,
> With our lamps all trimmed and bright?
> If, at the dawn of the early morning,
> He shall call us one by one,
> When to the Lord we restore our talents,
> Will He answer you, "Well done"?

DIFFICULT TIMES

I have shown in numerous places that the rub down here is obvious. Perhaps I see it more than ever since I've seen the mortal and immortal realms. At times we can have an overwhelming urge to cry for the Kingdom. I get it! Earthly life is hard, and Heaven is easy. Consider how much our faith ancestors had to bear up, before they could finally set one foot upon the beautiful Promised Land. Even though he was taken into the third heaven, Paul's difficulties were epic.

- He was confined to a jail cell (Acts 16:16-40).

- Shipwrecked, stranded on an island (Acts 27:15).

- Paul's people persecuted him (Acts 14:19) and constantly ran from those seeking to stone him. He was imprisoned toward the end of his life and beheaded (Acts 20:22-24).

We learn that the road from the earth to the Promised Land is often not straight or short. I am sure that you can attest to this. Life can be a hard-winding road filled with dangers, trials, and tribulations.

We must often pass through the wildernesses of pain, suffering, and loss. Not to mention that God can take us through the roundabout and indirect means. None of this is a demonic intrusion from within, but an outside failed world obtrusively evil, where the Kingdom suffers violence at the hands of violent men.

God is also sovereign and allows things to be sifted through His hands for our good, we cannot forget this. He chose not to lead the Israelites in a direct line straight from Egypt to Canaan but 200 miles around. Then He made them occupy desert wanderings for forty years, only to bring them into Canaan on the side furthest from Egypt. So it is with God, and our lives as God's people.

We learn that God will have us live on bread, but He does not make the bread for us. God creates the plant and leaves it to be nourished by the air and water to finally ripen so that it bears that beautiful golden grain to make bread to eat. God's way is to allow His children time to gather their experiences in life and learn to throw off habits that bind them.

We must often live under greater discipline, learn the art of war to gain steadiness and courage in the face of our enemies, all for a greater calling to come.

Finally, we are all born into a particular sphere with certain powers. Then God allows the circumstances of life to work within us. This takes place under divine supervision. Not that it hasn't occurred to you, but Yeshua Himself did not enter His ministry at once, but remained in obscurity for 30 years before His mission began. Moses was fit only after so many things had befallen him. He underwent training for 80 years. Then there are those difficulties inherent in life.

And so it is with this life of faith, we overcome, press in, and draw water when we are thirsty. He walks and talks with us, leveling our paths and strengthening our hearts for Him.

But God sent His Son to nest us here until He returns, or He takes us home.

18

LEARNING
THE "I" IN LIFE

ALL THAT I HAVE SHARED CONCERNING THE GLORY folds into a life of making the Great I Am your God! He is incomprehensible. He brings a hush upon all. Be still, O man, and listen. Be still, O vessel, and know. I AM God! This is the holy call to us. To return to Him as our only source—the I AM.

Returning to the Fountain of Life, our Source of Living Waters, your soul will be refreshed, and your spirit renewed. This is the divine call of an awakening that calls out to all of God's children: Return to My Presence which is found within—I AM! This chapter is about learning the "I" in life and what you must do in the moments ahead, preparing for your 30 Steps in 30 Days devotional.

I was 45 years old when I left my secular job, when I heard His voice that I should resign my position as vice president of a company with a six-figure salary in the early 1980s. That year we had just built a house with a high mortgage, and my oldest daughter had college in sight when I heard the Lord say that I needed to liquidate my savings and retirement and give it to ministries. He wanted to bring us down to zero, and we needed to learn a new level of faith.

Oh! Get ready for the new level of faith, He said. It's an adventure that you'll never forget. I'm sure that Abraham never forgot the time when he heard the voice of God tell him to leave his home with his family, and all his belongings for the Promised Land. I'm sure all the men and women in Hebrews 11, the great hall of fame of faith, lived with memories etched in their minds when they headed out. I confronted what I call "no man's land" because the supernatural is not fit for our humanity. It's never comforting. But I sensed my Father's arms tightening around me, the blood rushing to my face, my brain still trying to process it before my body could imagine what it would feel like. I remember the realization that I needed to deliver this news to my beautiful wife, following two decades of financial stability.

> We were about to embark upon an adventure to learn as Moses learned.

I will confess. That morning in New York, I wept briefly over this decision. But not over the loss of money. Although I had come to enjoy the work of my hands, it was too much to comprehend that He loved us so much that He was calling us to serve Him.

Our heavenly Father does not want our homes, jobs, or financial prosperity. He wants our hearts. That day I looked at my hands and said to my Father, "You are asking me to give up my ability to provide for my wife and children." He said, "Yes, but I will provide a new way." Then in my heart, I resigned myself to that I, and said to the Great I Am, "I will jump into Your hands, Lord." It's that simple and yet deeply profound.

Are you ready to conquer that unknown territory called "no man's land"? So many questions flood your mind at the breach of the no man's land and the life of Glory. You can't make sense of it. You're standing on the edge of certainty to your back and a world of uncertainty before you, as you look for the courage to jump into your Father's loving hands. You contemplate such things in nanoseconds as the risk factors are popping up in the mind.

It is interesting that a phone call came that evening from a client I had known for many years. I remember when the phone rang at 8 p.m. He explained that he was retiring and asked if I would be interested in moving to Long Island and taking over the company with his son. This business was well known and very prosperous. Quickly, I would have been a millionaire within five years. Bonnie and I looked at each other, knowing that this was a test of our hearts for service to the God of Heaven. We knew it! Then we laughed at the timing. Perhaps we laughed because of our nervousness, or a river of emotion that was being released, because we knew that the Great I AM had spoken. Well, the rest is history.

I promptly called him back to convey my appreciation for his offer and shared that my life was going in a different direction. When we jumped, what was solid and predictable became like sinking sand at first. A least it felt that way in the natural. Sound familiar? The questions are practical:

- How do I pay my bills, mortgage, and children's college?
- How do we get through each day, let alone the future?

NO MAN'S LAND

No man's land! The life of Glory, and a new life with the King of Glory. Wow! Its for you friend! As we go from glory to glory, and season to season, God has you in the palm of His hand. No man's land fits only the supernatural, that is why it's called no man's land. It's where the predictable and the solid turns soft, and you feel that your feet are in sinking sand. It's the moment when you will feel like the captain of the Starship Enterprise heading where you have never gone before; and the next, perhaps captain of the Titanic because everything feels like it's sinking.

What is this I? It is the I in: I do not understand what You are doing, Lord, but I will do Your will anyway. I says, I don't know what's ahead, Lord, but I will rest in You, Father. This I is the reach that I want you to take, as you take your apprehensions and uncertainties, and introducing them to the divine, I AM.

I will say, the transformational prayer life that I received on the glory side, was an enormous boost in these last three years of no-mans land. The activation of the spirit that ensued while praying heavens way throughout the years following my return, made it epic I will say. Absolutely fabulous!

Imagine going against the grain so acutely of not asking or petitioning, at a time that our natural inclination is to petition. But He said, no petition, praise, and thanksgiving for all that He has done. This season is dedicated to being a "lover" of Him only. "It's not about, I, me, Mine, and Our," He said. I want you to experience what the Lord said to me upon my return from Heaven:

> *"Let not your silence be tainted by desires, wants, and needs, for they will only distract you from the living present, I AM. Let no vague impressions of your past and shadowy images of the future lead you astray from what I desire for you. Rather, let your silence be receptive to the Light of My presence, for I am the Holy One of Israel who dissolves all tainted desires and thoughts. I invite you into an ocean rather than a stream. I want you to see me as the great I Am.*

To learn more about this heavenly prayer model, read *Heavens Soul Cleanse* and a *Rabbi's Journey to Heaven*.

CONCLUSION

MY PASTORAL HEART NOW COMPLETES MY JOURNEY WITH you, but I have reserved a couple of rough diamonds in the rough for you to polish along the way.

As we live in a world where covetousness is ambition, a deception that influences God's people. Don't chase this allusive wind just because the world sees hoarding as prudence and greed as industry. We are shoulder to shoulder with the very system counter to a sacred life. As a result, there isn't enough room and time for the Glory to move in many.

- What if God asks you to turn into that parking lot bustling with people? And He will! Will you make the time?

- God may want you to witness and pray for someone.

- Will you stay or will you go?

- Can you jettison your schedule for the Glory?

- Can you allow yourself to be moved by God for the purpose of giving glory to Him?

Your perspective will be the key to your success, as well as your desire. Participating in the Kingdom is first born out of your heart; it also means simplifying your life so that you can be activated and mobilized for Him. Stay intentional! That's how the glory activates. Remember, it's living close enough to the world where it has lost its pull and influence upon the soul—We are decreasing, and He is increasing.

I returned from Heaven, only to realize how much we have grossly underestimated the Glory of our Risen King. This has been such a deep motivational force in this book. The depth and breadth of His love exceed any human comprehension. The glory and the works of His hands are expressed day and night. So, explore it! Enjoy life in Him!

In celebrating your spiritual advancements ahead, we have studied the glory through wonderful examples of transformation born out of the glory side. Not through a formula, transaction, or clever principle, or end goal, but by way of life, and my time in Heaven. Through an inside-out relationship where you find a vibrant inward life cultivated by the Glory. It's about a habitation each day without limits. Get up in the morning with excitement, because you have learned to refuse the restrictions of convention and tradition. You've tasted what life is like under a limitless sky overhead.

With all the keys to living in His Glory at your disposal, you have learned the dance steps for *Dancing Past the Darkness*. It's almost as if we've walked endlessly together up to this point, where the former ways have become a smear and no longer definable. It's a long walk back that we don't want to take. Complete your spiritual dance now. Go and dance on top of that fast-moving train with grace and ease. Perhaps invite someone else to join you on top of that moving train. Start a movement!

I pray you will dance as unabashedly as David did before our King of Glory so you find the life of Glory and the adventure of Kingdom Normalcy!

30 Steps in 30 Days into Kingdom Normalcy

My time of recording my adventure has been completed. You are the soldier bride, and I can see the glimmer in your eyes. You may have felt on edge at times' precisely what I thought! We have also turned convention on it's head. So, perhaps we have done enough pinpricking here to last a long time.

You're about to go on an adventure, and my heart is racing, pondering your prospects for *Dancing Past the Darkness.* We have covered the necessary dance steps to enter a life of *Dancing Past the Darkness.* It will take some doing and mindfulness, but you will succeed. As *Heaven's Soul Cleanse* addressed the soul, the following addresses a pattern of living for a Glory mindset to remain. Steps are given that you can practice each day.

This is a 30-day adventure that gives a daily devotional and meditation to support you in a Glory mindset. You are taking diamonds in the rough to polish so they shine forth the Kingdom's Glory. All the points mentioned here have been a way of life following the Glory side, which began in September 2019.

Now take the 30 step devotional book, and begin you dance steps. Be sure to journal your daily adventure in the space provided in the devotional. Each morning starts with a daily a devotion and a daily action step. As days lead to weeks, you will be incorporating a life of Kingdom Normalcy once again. You are about to enter Kingdom life with others, following in the footsteps of the Messiah. To enrich your 30-day devotional, incorporate the *30-day Soul Cleanse*, and *A Rabbi's Journey to Heaven,* it marries beautifully with the entire process.

Note From Rabbi Felix

THANK YOU FOR THE PRIVILEGE OF SPEAKING INTO YOUR life, and for taking the time to read this work. May the Glory overshadow you, may His face shine upon you, may you find a river of His presence and a glory life to live for. Go out and get soaked by His rains. Worry not of what days are before us. Let no man put fear in your heart, and live a life that God intended for you.

Love in Messiah,
RABBI FELIX HALPERN

About The Author

Felix Halpern was born in 1952 in the Netherlands. As a child, his family immigrated to the United States, where he was raised in the northern New Jersey area. Before full-time ministry, he established a lucrative career in the precious metals and diamond industries at the International Diamond Center of New York City. Immersed for nearly two decades in the Orthodox and Hasidic Jewish communities, he gave his life to the salvation of the Jewish people.

Coming from a rich Jewish heritage, it is also rooted in Nazi resistance. Rabbi Halpern's paternal grandfather was an Orthodox rabbi and leader of his synagogue in Germany. His maternal grandparents established one of the many underground resistance movements against Hitler throughout the Netherlands. It is also where his father received the knowledge and understanding of his Messiah while being hidden with other Jews after miraculously escaping Germany.

MINISTRY TODAY

Today, Felix Halpern ministers nationally and internationally with a message of restoration between Jew and Gentile and an anointing of the evangelist. He serves as a nationally appointed missionary to the Jewish people. For twenty years, he and his wife, Bonnie, served as senior leaders of a Messianic congregation they founded, Beth Chofesh (House of Freedom).

He pioneered the first National Jewish Fellowship of the Assemblies of God and has served the first four years as its president. He has also served as a general presbyter for the Assemblies of God, on the AG Board of Ethnicity, and Lost Lamb Evangelistic Association board.

In 2013 God provided the means to form the first Resource Office for Jewish Ministry within the Assemblies of God in the greater New York and New Jersey metropolitan region, called Metro Jewish Resources.

In 2019, Rabbi Felix suffered a fatal heart attack to the malpractice of his doctor, experienced the supernatural crossing over as his body was dead, and experienced the Throne of God and life in the third heaven. God gave His life back, and following authored *A Rabbi's Journey to Heaven* and *Heaven's Soul Cleanse,* featured on Sid Roth ministries. His life and death experience and his journey into the third heaven established Chofesh Ministries (Freedom Ministries) in 2020.

CONTACT INFORMATION

WWW.CHOFESH.ORG

EMAIL: hisglobalglory@gmail.com

For Donations and Correspondence:
Felix Halpern
PO Box 3777
Wayne, NJ 07474

From

FELIX HALPERN

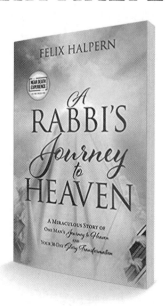

A Rabbi's Journey to Heaven

It all happened suddenly. In a twinkling of an eye. Rabbi Felix died, left his body, and crossed over into heaven. Amazed, he experienced the glories of heaven that he always read, pondered, and dreamt about. He also saw the lower realm, the second heaven, where demons dwell.

Three days after returning from heaven, God also gave Rabbi Felix a gift called "The Heavenly Soul Cleanse" which holds the keys to a transformational prayer life that turns our current prayer culture upside down. Rabbi Felix now lives from an open heaven, and as he shares these heavenly keys with you in this book, so will you. Imagine saturating your soul in heavenly glory and starving your soul from the natural order. As you do, God will heal your soul, and you will be launched into an entirely new operating system.

Take this journey with Rabbi Felix and experience this heavenly transformation. True freedom awaits you, and you will never be the same!

Purchase your copy wherever books are sold

From

FELIX HALPERN

30 Days of His Glory

It all happened suddenly. In a twinkling of an eye. Rabbi Felix died, left his body, and crossed over into heaven. Amazed, he experienced the glories of heaven that he had only read, pondered, and dreamt about.

In these extraordinary heavenly experiences, Rabbi Felix's eyes were opened to life-changing truths about the spiritual world that he shares with you.

Imagine submerging your soul in the Glory of God, and starving your soul of the natural for 30 days! For 30 days you will drown your soul in the Glory and magnification of God! You will experience heaven's operating system as it was given to Rabbi Felix. You will be launched into a daily living where you have a sky over your life and no longer a ceiling.

Heaven's Soul Cleanse is 100% biblical, and 100% centered upon the magnification and enlargement of God's glory and presence. It is guaranteed to imprint your soul and transform your mind. No longer will you be burdened by mortal pressures; no longer will you ask God repeatedly for the same thing. This new operating system will teach you to transfer ownership of your daily burdens to God, and it is 100% sustainable.

Purchase your copy wherever books are sold